Journal of Education for Students Placed At Risk

SPECIAL ISSUE
When Diversity Works: Bridging Families, Peers, Schools, and Communities at CREDE

GUEST EDITORS
Catherine Cooper and Patricia Gándara

Guest Editor's Introduction: When Diversity Works: Bridging Families,   1
Peers, Schools, and Communities at CREDE
Catherine Cooper and Patricia Gándara

School–Community-Based Organization Partnerships for Language   7
Minority Students' School Success
Carolyn Temple Adger

Finding Ways In: Community-Based Perspectives on Southeast Asian   27
Family Involvement With Schools in a New England State
Francine F. Collignon, Makna Men, and Serei Tan

Good or Bad? Peer Influences on Latino and European American   45
Adolescents' Pathways Through School
Margarita Azmitia and Catherine R. Cooper

Planning for the Future in Rural and Urban High Schools   73
Patricia Gándara, Dianna Gutiérrez, and Susan O'Hara

Latino Immigrant Parents and Children Learning and Publishing Together   95
in an After-School Setting
Richard Durán, Jane Durán, Deborah Perry-Romero, and Edith Sanchez

Bridging Funds of Distributed Knowledge: Creating Zones of Practices in   115
Mathematics
Norma González, Rosi Andrade, Marta Civil, and Luis Moll

Segregated Classrooms, Integrated Intent: How One School Responded to   133
the Challenge of Developing Positive Interethnic Relations
Rosemary C. Henze

COMMENTARIES

The Holographic Properties of Diversity   157
Gil N. Garcia

Building Bridges of Home, School, and Community: The Importance of   161
Design
Joyce L. Epstein

Notes on Contributors   169

JOURNAL OF EDUCATION FOR STUDENTS PLACED AT RISK, 6(1&2), 1–5
Copyright © 2001, Lawrence Erlbaum Associates, Inc.

Guest Editors' Introduction: When Diversity Works: Bridging Families, Peers, Schools, and Communities at CREDE

Catherine Cooper
University of California, Santa Cruz
Department of Psychology and Department of Education

Patricia Gándara
University of California, Davis
Division of Education

In industrialized countries, students' pathways through school to work have been described as an "academic pipeline." Democracies hold an ideal of access to educational opportunities by choice and advancement by merit, but in reality, as students move through primary and secondary school to college, the numbers of ethnic minority and low-income youth in the academic pipeline shrink. The seven studies in this volume, all conducted through the Center for Research on Education, Diversity, and Excellence (CREDE), address the academic pipeline problem by focusing on three key themes: (a) involving all families in their children's schooling; (b) identifying ways the academic pipeline can be kept open for diverse students; and (c) helping students bridge their worlds of families, peers, schools, and communities.

The approaches found in these seven studies illuminate students' social worlds with multilevel, developmental perspectives on students, their relationships, institutional settings, and cultural communities. Rather than seeing diversity as a liability or deficit from the mainstream, this new "cultural bridges" research reveals

Requests for reprints should be sent to Catherine Cooper, Psychology Department, Social Sciences II, University of California, Santa Cruz, CA 95064. E-mail: ccooper@cats.ucsc.edu

both resources and challenges by mapping the factors—personal, relational, institutional, and cultural—that help students navigate across their worlds and stay in the academic pipeline. Both qualitative and quantitative approaches are used by these researchers, often in the same study. We envision this volume contributing to both policy and practice in local, state, and national settings where concerns for making diversity work are at the top of schools' and youth organizations' agendas.

In the articles by Adger and by Collignon, Men, and Tan, the authors map the terrain of community-based organizations (CBOs) that work with diverse communities and elucidate how one such organization serving Southeast Asian immigrants helps bridge mainstream and immigrant cultural forms and structures. These articles add richly to a meager literature on community-based organizations and their contributions as cultural brokers and critical support systems. Adger surveyed 31 organizations and conducted site visits at 17 to provide descriptive analyses of (a) the types of CBOs that partner with schools; (b) the nature of the partnerships that are forged; (c) the kinds of work that they do; and (d) the factors that contribute to success and failure in these relationships. Adger finds that relationships between partnerships and schools vary from integrated to complementary. Partnerships ran alternative schools, full-service schools, and programs complementing schools' academic programs. The work that partnerships do varies across students' age and grade. At preschool through middle school, partnerships often focus on parent and family involvement in children's education and provide social services to ensure children are prepared for and supported through school by family and community. At the secondary level, partnerships provide tutoring, school-to-work internships, and programs promoting leadership skills and higher education goals; they also discourage pregnancy and drugs that mitigate educational success for these students.

Collignon and her colleagues focus on Cambodian, Laotian, Hmong, and Vietnamese students in Rhode Island schools. Students from these communities are at risk of educational failure because of differences between the expectations of the schools and students' languages, cultural practices, socioeconomic status, and other legacies of war in their families' homelands. The study examines (a) factors in the multiple cultures—home, school and community—of Southeast Asian students in Rhode Island which prevent or promote their academic achievement; and (b) features of collaborations between community- and school-based programs, which impact school achievement. The work of the CBO is based on a belief that, by working together, these entities can provide value-added services to students and families in the target population. Their joint activities broker understanding of effective educational practices across generations, languages, and cultures. To focus on student achievement and benefits from these relationships, the project initially sought data about Southeast Asian populations. Finding little, the project generated its own, thereby building a foundation for both understanding and evaluating the community's needs and the effectiveness of the organization in meeting those needs. To make transparent how such an organization promotes its goals, the article describes a specific activity setting for studying features of productive partnerships supporting student success: the Southeast Asian Summer Academy of the Socio-Economic Development Center for Southeast Asians (SEDC) in the Providence School District.

The articles by Azmitia and Cooper and by Gándara, Gutiérrez, and O'Hara focus on European American and Latino adolescents as they journey through adolescence in middle and high schools. Both articles take a developmental perspective, analyzing students' attitudes, relationships, and achievement over time. These articles trace how families, peers, communities, and schools interact with these students to both support and impede their academic progress and aspirations. Azmitia and Cooper put the question succinctly: Are peers good or bad for the academic outcomes of Latino and European American youth? They find that the answer to this question is that they are both—good *and* bad. Their critical contribution is in describing *how* peers affect the academic trajectories of their fellow students and in suggesting what schools and programs can do to tip the balance in favor of good. Azmitia and Cooper describe the increasing solidarity that students in special academic programs come to feel with other students who have shared the same experiences over time. Shared experiences and shared goals can provide the basis for supportive and affirming peer relations that lead to successful postsecondary outcomes.

Gándara and her colleagues investigate the differences in the ways that Latino and European American youth experience schooling, peers, and relationships with parents over the critical identity-forming years of high school in a rural and an urban high school. The authors find that the context of schooling—rural or urban—exerts a significant influence on the formation of postsecondary aspirations, independent of ethnicity. Thus, on some dimensions, the fact that a student is Latino or White is less important than that she goes to school in a rural environment. Risks are also very different in these two environments. The urban environment offers all the traditional risks that strike terror in the hearts of parents—drugs, alcohol, pressure for sexual experimentation, and gang activity. But the somewhat more protected rural environment, in which there are no anonymous students, offers its own kind of risks—ignorance of opportunity and restricted visions of the "possible self." Ultimately, however, being a student of color adds additional risks and limits academic opportunity. Gándara and her colleagues explore these risk factors and describe ways students attempt to construct their academic identities through the eyes of their peers, families, and communities.

The articles by Durán, Durán, Perry-Romero, and Sanchez and by González, Andrade, Civil, and Moll shift the focus from the school as the context of activity to the community. Each article looks at structured activities in the community that have the potential to contribute, sometimes in unexpected ways, to the academic competencies of Latino youth. Durán and his colleagues describe a project centered on developing computer-based literacy and empowerment for low-income Latino parents and their school children. Small groups of parents were invited to participate and interact with their children on computers in an after-school setting. In addition to documenting the process of helping parents learn skills to support their children's learning, the project sought to evaluate the extent to which parents also learned practical computer skills. Pre- and post-project assessments showed statistically significant gains in parents' knowledge of computers. Embedded formative performance assessments, ethnographic data, field notes, and video data were also used to trace processes through which parents and children worked together to learn technology skills and apply them to publishing. As parents and children were guided with planning, drafting, writing and editing computer-based texts in joint publication, the project itself became a new community-based organization fostering literacy and bridging community, homes, and schools. Thus, the Duran et al. article points the way to an innovative model for involving parents in their children's education, while profiting the experience themselves in very tangible ways.

González and her colleagues offer an example of how community knowledge can be tapped to strengthen the academic experiences of Latino youth. Drawing on the long-term study of "funds of knowledge" in local communities, González and her colleagues apply the model to an investigation of the mathematical potential of Latino households. The authors describe ways women participating in a sewing circle use and model sophisticated mathematical knowledge that might otherwise be unacknowledged by schools and even by their own children. They find that the same women who may be viewed as lacking the competency to help their children in the study of mathematics in fact use mathematical concepts in their daily work. The authors note, however, that, whereas other classroom knowledge domains such as literacy and language arts may draw in a rather straightforward fashion from households, mathematical knowledge may not be so easily incorporated. Thus, the article investigates the ways in which household mathematical knowledge may be translated into practices that support children's academic development. In so doing, this work contributes significantly to our understanding the potential for families and communities to be involved in practical ways in supporting the educational trajectories of diverse youth.

Finally, Henze focuses on broader themes of racial prejudice, segregation, and the potential for schools to serve as allies in the quest for better inter-group relations. Henze poses the question whether schools *can* serve such a function, given their history of social reproduction of inequality, and notes that she is not alone in questioning whether this is a realistic possibility. Nonetheless, she describes the experience of "Cornell" school, which deals simultaneously with the need to provide language instruction for children who do not speak English sufficiently well to access the core curriculum and the need to integrate children across ethnic groups to break down tensions and suspicions fostered by segregation. Henze points out the real tensions between competing goals and methods that have no easy resolution. However, she also describes innovative classroom teaming and parent involvement classes that allow parents, as well as students, the opportunity to come to know each other across ethnic lines. Her message is one of realism, but also of hope. Henze suggests that by paying attention to the difficult task of bridging families, schools, and communities we can, indeed, create a more equitable society, and that schools may play a significant role in this enterprise.

In each of their commentaries on this special issue, García and Epstein enrich our perspectives by placing the seven studies in broader context of emerging coalitions among researchers, policymakers, educators, and community members. García juxtaposes examples of innovative diversity policies and practices in corporate business with the studies of this volume to illuminate the multidimensional "holographic" processes that build communities as full partnerships among their stakeholders. Epstein's thoughtful analysis of designing bridges across home, school, and community delineates some of the new structures, processes, and practices available from the Center for Research on Education, Diversity, and Excellence, the National Network of Partnership Schools, and other coalitions on behalf of diverse students, families, and communities. We hope this volume stimulates the further growth of such coalitions.

ACKNOWLEDGMENTS

This work was supported under the Education Research and Development Program, PR/Award No. R306A60001, the Center for Research on Education, Diversity and Excellence (CREDE), as administered by the Office of Educational Research and Improvement (OERI), National Institute on the Education of At-Risk Students (NIEARS), U.S. Department of Education (USDoE).

We thank Courtney Cazden, Fred Erickson, and Evelyn Jacob for their guidance of the program on Families, Peers, Schools, and Communication of CREDE, and Sam Stringfield, Amanda Datnow, and Tiffany Meyers for their help with this volume.

The contents, findings and opinions expressed here are those of the authors and do not necessarily represent the positions or policies of OERI, NIEARS, or the USDoE.

JOURNAL OF EDUCATION FOR STUDENTS PLACED AT RISK, 6(1&2), 7–25

School–Community-Based Organization Partnerships for Language Minority Students' School Success

Carolyn Temple Adger

Center for Applied Linguistics
Washington, DC

Because language minority students, including immigrants and the U.S.-born children of immigrants, may have to contend with a mismatch between the language and culture of their schools and those of their communities, as well as the schools' difficulty in addressing their academic needs appropriately, some schools have been partnering with community-based organizations (CBOs) to broaden the base of support for these students. This article outlines findings from a study of school–CBO partnerships that promote the academic achievement of language minority students. It describes the types of CBOs that partner with schools, the ways partners work together, and the work that they do. Crucial elements in program success are discussed, as well as challenges that partnerships may face.

Educators and researchers alike have recognized that school and family-based interventions alone cannot provide every student with the support needed for academic success (Rutherford & Billig, 1995). For language minority students, including immigrants and the U.S.-born children of immigrants, a mismatch between the language and culture of the schools and those of students' communities can make school success difficult. If school systems do not address their academic needs appropriately, these students are placed at risk for poor performance and school failure. Partnerships between community-based organizations (CBOs) and schools

---

Requests for reprints should be sent to Carolyn Temple Adger, Center for Applied Linguistics, 4646 40th Street, N.W., Washington, DC 20016. E-mail: Carolyn@cal.org

Portions of this article are from *Broadening the Base: School/Community Partnerships Serving Language Minority Students At-Risk,* by C. T. Adger and J. Locke, 2000, Educational Practice Report. University of California, Santa Cruz: Center for Research on Education, Diversity and Excellence. Reprinted with permission.

have been recommended as vehicles to assist students in achieving academic success (Davis, 1991; Dryfoos, 1994a, 1994b; Heath, 1993; Heath & McLaughlin, 1987, 1991; Jones, 1992; Kirst, 1991; National Coalition of Advocates for Students, 1994; Perrone, 1993; Price, Gioci, Penner, & Trautlein, 1993; Roth & Hendrickson, 1991; Seeley, 1984). Such partnerships are currently connecting schools directly with the community and assisting students in ways that go beyond the schools' traditional methods. However, little is known about those that serve language minority students and the programs they provide, what makes them effective, and how their experiences might benefit others (Davis, 1991; Price et al., 1993). This article presents findings from a study of partnerships considered to be successful in promoting the academic achievement of language minority students. It describes the types of CBOs that partner with schools, the partnerships that they forge, and the work that they do, as well as their perceptions of what makes their programs successful.

METHOD

The findings reported here come from a national survey of school–CBO partnerships perceived as effective in serving language minority students and from site visits to 17 of them. One hundred partnerships were identified by advocacy organizations (e.g., the National Coalition of Advocates for Students), regional comprehensive centers, regional laboratories, and state departments of education, and in response to requests for nomination posted on three listservs and the Web site of the Center for Applied Linguistics (CAL). All nominees were contacted by telephone and asked to provide information about their programs. Sixty-two programs were selected for study: All support students' academic improvement and all serve preschool to college-age students and their families. All of them offer long-term programs for students and families from language minority backgrounds—those for whom English is not the first language.

Definitions

Early interactions with individuals concerned with school–CBO partnerships led to elaboration of key constructs. These understandings shaped development of the survey and the guiding questions for site visits.

CBOs.   CBOs are groups that are committed to helping people obtain health, education, and other basic human services. Many but not all CBOs are legally constituted nonprofit organizations with tax-exempt status under Section 501(c)(3) of the Internal Revenue Code. Organizations from outside the community that cooperate with schools to support learning were considered beyond the scope of this study. For example, museums do not conform to the core meaning of CBOs. They operate outreach programs that contribute to students' intellectual development, but their focus is not on basic human services.

Academic achievement. Interactions with individuals involved in school–CBO partnerships and their programs—telephone conversations, surveys, and site visits—suggested that programs focused on supporting students' school success, a construct including academic achievement but also extending beyond that. Certain attitudes, abilities, and actions are essential for students (e.g., taking leadership in school and community, staying in school, and meeting graduation requirements) because without these factors, academic achievement is moot. Partnerships promote the value of education and the attitudes and actions associated with being successful at school and also support academic achievement as it is traditionally viewed—learning academic content and demonstrating knowledge—often in the form of highly personalized tutoring. They view their work, and it is viewed by others, as providing the broad base of support that students need to progress through school.

Program success. A third construct for definition is partnership and program success. This study did not undertake to evaluate the programs provided by the school–CBO partnerships it identified. Instead, it accepted the judgments of individuals and entities concerned with educating language minority students. Survey respondents were asked to provide evidence of program effectiveness and to account for their success. Analysis of their responses was informed by further discussions during the site visits.

The Survey

To collect basic descriptive information that could inform schools and organizations seeking to create partnerships, a survey was developed, pilot tested, and mailed in early 1997 to 62 school–CBO partnerships that had been nominated. This survey concerns the structure and the functions of the partnerships. It requests information about the programs that partnerships provide—their design, goals, funding sources, evaluation techniques and results, constituents, and services provided—the challenges they face, and indicators of their success. It also elicits features of the partnerships themselves. To encourage survey completion, respondents were offered copies of the project's products and a research or educational practice report from the Center for Research on Education, Diversity, and Excellence. Despite extensive telephone follow-up, the response rate for this survey was only 50% ($n = 31$). On the phone, partnership staff members explained that they do not take time for paperwork that is not essential to their functioning. Table 1 lists the partnerships responding to the survey. (Information about the sites comes from public documents, surveys, and site visits. That which is not public is used with written permission.)

The follow-up telephone conversations revealed a weakness in the survey instrument. It assumes that programs and partnerships are more institutionalized than is often the case. The following question serves as an example: "How many students in total are directly served by the program?" Interviews during the site visits revealed that partnerships have a general knowledge of how many clients are being served at any time, but clients come and go frequently so that counts may not be accurate. Moreover, many CBOs, understaffed and underfunded, give record keeping short shrift. Several individuals expressed impatience with questions like this one that seemed tangential to their mission and accomplishments.

The Site Visits

For a more detailed picture of school–CBO partnerships and their programs, 17 site visits were conducted. The sites (indicated by boldface in Table 1) included a range of types of CBOs, types of partnership structures, program goals, demographics, and locations—California, Florida, Maryland, Massachusetts, New York, Texas, and Washington. Data from these visits include extensive field notes detailing interviews with program directors, coordinators, service providers, and other staff from the programs, CBOs, schools, and other participating organizations—as well as detailed accounts of program activities observed. Field notes were stored electronically, coded, sorted, and analyzed for reporting, following traditional qualitative research procedures (Erickson, 1986). Program reports, videos, and informational brochures were also collected and reviewed.

Findings from data analysis are summarized in the following sections describing the types of CBOs that partner with schools to promote school success for language minority students at risk, the nature of the partnerships, the characteristics of the programs that they provide, and elements that make programs effective.

RESULTS

Types of CBOs That Partner With Schools

Three kinds of CBOs partner with schools to support language minority students: ethnic organizations, special-purpose CBOs, and multipurpose CBOs. *Ethnic organizations* serve a general culture-brokering function for the school, the students,

TABLE 1
School–CBO Partnerships

Program	Location	Year Started	Program Functions
Academic Youth Employment Program	Toppenish, WA	1987	Provides tutoring and career exploration for migrant and at-risk youth.
ACCESS	Dearborn, MI	1977	Provides bilingual community resources such as health services, family counseling, vocational education, cultural arts programs, adult education, and mental health and social services.
Alum Rock Even Start Program	San Jose, CA	1991	Provides literacy and parenting classes for adults and early childhood programs for children.
ASPIRA	Miami, FL	1992	Operates an alternative middle school for at-risk students, particularly Puerto Rican, Latino, and Haitian.
Bell Cluster Healthy Start Collaborative	Bell, CA	1995	Improves student achievement by addressing health and counseling needs; provides tutoring and mentoring.
Cambridge City Links	Cambridge, MA	1992	Introduces linguistic minority youth to government careers and trains them for leadership positions in the community through public sector apprenticeships, public service career seminars, and replication.
Castelar Healthy Start	Los Angeles, CA	1984	Addresses human service needs of families and children in the community through case management, health care, parenting classes, and so on. Also addresses domestic violence, substance abuse, and gang-related issues.
Challenger Center	Adelphi, MD	1993	Combines interagency resources to ensure the well-being of young children and their families and communities. Family centers provide tutoring, teacher–parent conferences, ESL classes, and other services.

(continued)

TABLE 1
(Continued)

Program	Location	Year Started	Program Functions
Children's Aid Society Community Schools	New York, NY	1991	Strengthens the educational process for teachers, parents, and students through health counseling, recreation, and education for the entire family.
Colonias Project	El Paso, TX	1990	Builds community centers in impoverished border communities and supports development of programs that provide social services, connect schools and communities, and help students learn English.
Community Achievement Project in the Schools	New York, NY	1990	Brokers partnerships between schools and CBOs to enhance students' well-being, attendance, and academic performance.
Community Service Learning	Springfield, MA	1988	Provides tutoring and mentoring integrated with the school curriculum.
Cuban-American National Council	Miami, FL	1987	Runs four alternative schools for Latino youth in trouble. The program attempts to turn disconnected and underachieving youth into successful students.
Filipino Youth Empowerment Project	Seattle, WA	1995	Provides tutoring, mentoring, and leadership training for high school students.
Junior National Health Service Corps	Kansas City, KS	1995	Introduces Latino youth from migrant or other poorly paid families to careers in medicine that serve the communities; assists in improving reading, writing, and spoken English skills.
Language Acquisition and Transition Program	Houston, TX	1996	Offers ESL instruction and vocational skills and supports students' academic development.

(continued)

TABLE 1
(Continued)

Program	Location	Year Started	Program Functions
Lennox/Hughes/UCLA Partnership	Lennox, CA	1992	Prepares families for young children's entry into school and prepares high school students for higher education and careers. Supports hands-on science and technology activities, English and native language instruction, after-school activities, and counseling in intergroup relations. Also strives to reduce problematic behaviors and improve health.
Liberty Partnerships Program	South Bronx, NY	1989	Provides support services to at-risk students; designed to increase students' motivation and ability to complete secondary education and to seek entry into postsecondary education and the workforce.
Migrant Education Even Start	Kansas City, KS	1996	Offers ESL literacy instruction to parents and children.
Modesto Healthy Start Program	Modesto, CA	1992	Provides comprehensive, integrated school-based and school-linked services to families.
Mother–Daughter Program	El Paso, TX	1986	Supports mother–daughter teams in setting and working toward higher education goals.
Murchison Family Center	Los Angeles, CA	1991	Helps students and families access health and support services to minimize barriers to learning.
New Beginnings	San Diego, CA	1988	Promotes family and community well-being through risk prevention and early academic intervention services.
Pacoima Urban Village	Pacoima, CA	1990	Provides comprehensive services for children and families and acts as a community center for adults; also is involved with curriculum and instruction at the school.
Project Achieve/Theodore Roosevelt High School: St. Rita's Center for Immigrants and Refugees	Bronx, NY	1989	Facilitates student transition into high school.

(continued)

TABLE 1
(Continued)

Program	Location	Year Started	Program Functions
Project Look: Learning Outreach Organization for Kids	Seattle, WA	1992	Provides academic and social services to disadvantaged children and families in low-income housing complexes.
Refugee and Immigrant Forum	Everett, WA	1979	Offers tutoring for at-risk immigrant youth from many countries.
School of the Future	Houston, TX	1987	Provides site-based counseling support services, violence prevention programs, drug prevention education, parent services, and community collaboration.
South East Regional Resource Center	Alaska	1976	Provides preschool and infant learning projects, family literacy programs, adult basic education, and postsecondary training in rural Alaska.
Transforming Education for New York's Newest	New York, NY	1996	Supports New York City schools in their efforts to respond to immigrant students through inservice professional development modules for teachers.
Vocational Building Skills, Inc.	Sanders, AZ	1983 and 1989	Serves Navajo, Hopi, and White Mountain Apache tribes/nations; trains high school and GED graduates for jobs that are available in the area, especially carpentry and computer technology.

Note. Boldface indicates programs visited. CBOs = community-based organizations; ESL = English as a second language; GED = general equivalency diploma.

and their families. They also provide programs. For example, the Filipino Community Center in Seattle, Washington, runs the Filipino Youth Empowerment project that promotes leadership skills and helps students plan for higher education. It also helps parents understand the U.S. educational system and confront the issues affecting Filipino students in U.S. society. The *special-purpose CBO* operates one program. For example, the University of Texas at El Paso, Texas, organized a CBO to partner with a school district in running the Hispanic Mother/Daughter Program aimed at increasing the number of Hispanic girls going to college. The most common type of CBO is the *multipurpose CBO,* which provides more than one program. The Chinatown Service Center in Los Angeles operates the Castelar Healthy Start program, offering tutoring for students and health and other services for families at Castelar Elementary School. At other locations, it operates a community health clinic and social services, counseling, and employment programs.

The Dynamic Nature of School–CBO Partnerships

School–CBO partnerships tend to be structurally variable and fluid. They may include one or more schools or districts, one or more CBOs, as well as other organizations—colleges and universities and businesses. Federal, state, and local government agencies also play a partnership role in making social and other services available through the partnership or by providing funding. Partnerships often begin with a single project and add new program areas or expand those they have as new partners join. Groups also leave the partnership, usually because of the loss of funding. Each partnership studied had a history of changing partners and modifying programs. Project Look, in Seattle, Washington, demonstrates this. This partnership operates three "apartment schools" in apartment complexes located near elementary schools serving low-income language minority students (Russian, Latino, Cambodian, Vietnamese, and Pacific Islander students). These schools provide a safe place for students in Grades 1 through 6 to stay after school and get help with homework and tutoring in English or their first languages. The project began in 1992 as a collaboration between one school and a university with funding from a state grant to support the academic achievement of language minority students at risk. Six years later, 35 agencies had joined the partnership, including the school district, the public health and mental health departments of the local government, local libraries, two community colleges, the Rotary Club, the police department, and several CBOs. Through these partners, Project Look provides programs at the original site and two additional sites to prevent risky behavior (e.g., drug and alcohol use), violence, and dropping out. In addition, the CBO provides various programs and social services for parents.

Many (45%) of the respondents indicated that their partners maintain close connections, conferring frequently and making decisions jointly. In other cases (39%), such as Project Look, one of the partners (in this case a CBO) leads the work, and the others provide space and resources (e.g., tutors, workshop facilitators, and materials). Partners meet at regular intervals. Other respondents characterized their partners' connection in terms of coordinated services. Overall, the site visits suggested cordial relationships, although some partnerships had endured periods of conflict.

Functions of School–CBO Partnerships

Survey results showed that all of the school–CBO partnerships address students' academic achievement and all serve multiple functions. These include preparing parents for their child's schooling or increasing parental involvement in school (84%), reducing behaviors that interfere with schooling (e.g., substance abuse, dropping out, and truancy; 74%), preparing students for work (68%), involving the community in public education (65%), supporting students' preparation for higher education (65%), improving students' English language proficiency (61%), improving instruction (55%), and improving intergroup relations (55%).

Program foci vary with students' ages and grades. At the preschool through elementary school level, partnerships often focus on parents. Their programs help families prepare children for school activities and support their progress there. Related social services help parents—especially immigrants—develop English language and literacy skills and find jobs. However, partnerships also accomplish ambitious, comprehensive change so that elementary schools address the education and wellness of the whole student in the context of the family. For example, a partnership involving the Children's Aid Society and the New York City Public Schools made possible a new school building and program at Salome Urena (Intermediate School 218) in the Washington Heights neighborhood. At the secondary level, partnerships emphasize tutoring to help students succeed in their classes and develop English or other language skills, preparation for postsecondary education and work, and social development.

Core and Periphery

Some school–CBO programs operate at the academic core of the school program; others augment it. Three partnerships operate schools or programs within schools that weave together academic and other elements in school success. Dade County Public Schools (Miami, FL) contracts with the local ASPIRA (a national organization dedicated to developing better educated, more community-conscious and committed Latino and minority youth) and the Cuban National Council (CNC; a Miami-based group whose goal is to turn disconnected and underachieving youngsters into students). These organizations run small (fewer than 200 students) alternative schools for at-risk students, most of them from language minority backgrounds. Although their curriculum is the same as that of other schools, they also emphasize self-discipline and identity. The principal of CNC's Little Havana Institute described the acclimation process at that school. During the first academic year, students come to regard themselves as members of the school community. During the second year, they become academically engaged: They come to class prepared, and they participate. Standardized test scores begin rising in that year. The Houston Independent School District contracts with the Employment and Training Centers (a for-profit CBO) to operate the Language Acquisition and Transition Program at four high schools, helping new immigrants and students with a history of school problems develop their English skills and complete requirements for graduation or the general equivalency diploma (GED) as they learn job skills.

Other partnerships augment the school program by providing academic support. At the South Bronx High School in New York City, a summer remedial program put together by the South Bronx Overall Economic Development Corporation (a CBO) evolved into a year-round tutoring program for language minority and other students having academic difficulty. The program, which is now a New York State Liberty Partnerships Program, also offers job training and placement.

Many programs add a strong cultural focus to academic support functions. For example, the Haitian Centers Council, a New York City CBO, provides Haitian staff for the guidance offices at Erazmus Hall High School in Brooklyn to advise Haitian students on academic and other matters. Because they know the language and culture of the students and the community, as well as that of the school, staff members can illuminate problem situations for students, families, and school staff that they might not be able to solve on their own. Other Haitian Centers Council offerings at the school are tutoring, workshops on risk avoidance and access to higher education, and social events.

Full-service schools represent another configuration of the schools' and the partnerships' work. Characteristically they provide educational programs for students and parents, as well as comprehensive health and social services. Salome Urena, mentioned earlier, is one of these. Many of the Healthy Start sites in California and the Even Start sites across the country offer health services (mental health, medical, dental, eye exams, etc.), programs for parents (e.g., English as a second language [ESL], GED, parenting classes, and family literacy), and early childhood programs at the school site. Colocation of services enhances opportunities for parents, school and other program staff, and students to know each other so that appropriate program placement and services can be negotiated.

Other programs have looser connections to the schools. The Filipino Youth Empowerment Program in Seattle functions independently, but schools contact the Program when academic or social problems arise with Filipino students. The Program's director confers with high school principals and guidance counselors frequently; students involved with the Program set up informational centers during school lunch hours to answer questions, publicize Program events such as weekend retreats on developing leadership skills, and distribute brochures describing the Program's peer mentoring and tutoring services.

Partnerships provide a range of programs and services suited to the settings in which they work. Whatever work they do, the partnerships' overall goal is to broaden the base of support so that language minority students can be successful at school.

PROGRAM SUCCESS

What does it take to fulfill the partnership's mission to support the school success of language minority students? The survey asked respondents to list features of their partnerships and programs that help to explain their reputations for effectiveness. This topic was introduced during site visits as well. Analysis of these data identified four program elements that practitioners find essential to program success: adequate resources, partnership and program flexibility, responsiveness to the clients, and evaluation. These elements are consistent with the findings from a study by the National Coalition of Advocates for Students (1994) that identified elements of responsiveness: a design that is appropriate for the constituency, accessible services, and use of the constituents' abilities. The study reported here identified three additional elements of success from the partnerships' perspective.

Resources

Partnership and program success depends on availability of resources over time. Essential resources include staff, funding, space, and materials.

Staff.   In all of the partnerships we visited, strong, committed, competent, and often charismatic individuals play key roles as partnership director, school program or CBO leader, program director, or service provider. They inspire other staff members and clients, and in the cases studied, they provide the stable core that preserves the staff and the programs over time (Dryfoos, 1998). At the Refugee and Immigrant Forum (Everett, WA), a staff member said of the director, "She is our strength," referring to the director's respect for all of the immigrant groups she works with, not just her own.

In addition to strong leadership, effective partnerships have capable staff members who work with clients. Hiring guidelines emphasize credentials, experience, language skills, and training, but most of these staff members also share their clients' backgrounds. For example, the Alum Rock Healthy Start Program in San Jose, California, employs immigrant women who have overcome many of the same social and educational challenges faced by the parents and children with whom they work. Thus they serve as role models for parents who may have few social contacts outside their immigrant community, as well as culture brokers linking the clients and the schools. They can provide appropriate services and the personalized help that keeps clients engaged in the programs. One of the program leaders told the story of a single mother who was unkempt and unable to control her young children, so other mothers avoided her in parenting and ESL classes. A client liaison worked with this mother to help her regain control. Program leaders believe that this intervention may have saved her from social isolation and her children from serious trouble later on.

Site visits revealed that staff members sometimes have long-standing personal ties to the programs and partnerships with which they work. At the Filipino Youth Empowerment Project in Seattle, young adults who are products of the project's early years, some of them former gang members, serve as Youth Advocates for current clients. Tutors for the Refugee and Immigrant Forum in Everett, Washington, once utilized the Forum's services for English language learners themselves. Several staff members at the Bell Cluster Healthy Start Center in California grew up in the community that the program serves. They graduated from the high school where the Center is located, along with some of the teachers and social service providers with whom they now work. One of the Haitian Center Council's staff members graduated from the school where she works. These staff members' rich knowledge of the local communities and schools adds depth and veracity to the programs.

Funding.   Dependable income is crucial to program success, but this is the greatest challenge facing all of the partnerships, even those like the one involving the Chinatown Service Center in Los Angeles that has maintained funding for more than 27 years. Unlike schools, which are assured of academic program stability despite fluctuating funding, most school–CBO partnerships can count on funding only for the duration of their current grants. In response to a question about adequate funding to keep programs operating for 2 to 3 years, five respondents indicated that they could not count on funding that far ahead.

Financial support for the partnerships comes from many sources. Eighteen of the partnerships receive federal government funding, commonly from Title I, Even Start, Medicare, and Department of Housing and Urban Development. Americorps volunteers work at the Refugee and Immigrant Forum. States provide funds to 22 programs; for example, California funds the Healthy Start Programs. Local governments contribute to 18 partnerships. National and local foundation funding goes to 15. For example, the Kellogg Foundation contributes to the Hispanic Mother/Daughter Program in El Paso, Texas.

Space and supplies.   Space and supplies were not among the partnerships' main concerns, perhaps because almost all of the projects studied were fairly well established. Space was mentioned by only two respondents to a survey question on "important features of your partnership that make it successful." All had managed to secure space for their programs and administrative functions, often in schools. Although some of it was less than desirable—for example, in one program, an ESL class for parents met on a school's stage—some was new or newly renovated. No one mentioned materials in the survey. Interviews suggested that finding space and supplies had been of concern at the time of program start-up or expansion but that it did not demand the same attention over time as did funding and staffing.

Flexibility

The fluid nature of school–CBO partnerships discussed earlier is a defining factor in their success from the practitioners' standpoint. Partners and their programs come and go, and partnerships must adjust to survive. They are able to do so because they are far less institutionalized than schools, subject to fewer external policies, and not held to long-standing traditions. All of the partnerships studied were less than 10 years old. Asked for advice for new partnerships, one staff member said this: "Don't look for immediate results. ... Expect that change demands partnerships to offer flexible solutions to problems."

Responsiveness of Design

Partnerships and programs that are flexible can respond to needs and new opportunities. The three facets of responsiveness identified by the National Coalition of Advocates for Students (1994) were apparent in this study's results.

1. *Appropriateness.* Program designs are appropriate for the users. Because these programs target language minority students, linguistic congruence and cultural appropriateness are essential. All of the partnerships and programs studied consider this matter fundamental. They address it by hiring staff members who share clients' linguistic and cultural heritage and who recognize their experiences in and out of schools. These staff members are able to develop the trusting relationships with clients that encourage program participation. These relationships are more personal than typical teacher–student–family relationships, which have a professional basis, but they are similar in that program staff members take an authoritative stance toward the client based on experience, enculturation, and training.

An important dimension of the programming that school–CBO partnerships offer is attention to the whole person, which each of the respondents mentioned. Schools cannot take this approach. Their mandate is promoting cognitive development. However, through partnerships with CBOs and other organizations, schools' academic focus is complemented by partners' missions. No partner brings all of the knowledge and resources necessary to support young people's development. In combination, however, they can define and deliver services that children need to perform their roles as students. Nonetheless, as several survey respondents pointed out, partnerships' capacity to help young people is not limitless. Social problems that bear on school success, such as violence, anti-immigrant sentiment in society, and changes in welfare and other social policy, present significant challenges to partnerships. In this regard, the efforts of the Filipino Youth Empowerment Project to help young people thrive in a dangerous society by reducing gang participation and supporting their academic progress illuminate the possibilities for designing programs that consider the students' social context broadly.

2. *Accessibility.* Successful programs are accessible to clients both physically and psychologically. Clients must feel comfortable in the program setting or they will not participate. Transportation to program sites can be a problem. The Alum Rock Even Start program addresses this challenge by offering parenting and ESL programs for mothers at the school buildings at the start of the school day when the mothers bring their children to school. The program also provides school-like day care for preschoolers so that the mothers can participate in activities and the children can be introduced to school routines. The mothers are also welcomed by the school principals or other administrators who talk to them in Spanish about their children's schoolwork and the value of their participation in their children's education.

3. *Building on abilities.* All of the programs show clients that school success is possible—that students have what it takes to succeed there. In a phone conversation (as part of follow-up to increase survey completion), the director of Nosotros Consulting, a CBO that works with migrant students in partnership with the Mabton, Washington, school district, pointed out that the all-too-common view of the immigrant student as *pobrecito* (poor little thing) is neither accurate nor constructive. He finds that schools too often coddle nontraditional students, killing their chances for success, and that, instead, schools should challenge students and coach them toward success. Nosotros Consulting's program tutors high school students and helps them accrue credits toward graduation or the GED. Similarly, at the Pacoima Urban Village in Pacoima, California, staff members asserted that every constituent, adult and child, is a member of the school–community partnership and that the partnership's goal is to develop the members' capacity to succeed in school and elsewhere.

Evaluation

Effective partnerships monitor their programs' results and use what they learn to celebrate their success and improve their services. High-quality programs have clear goals for their work, and they record their progress in reaching them.

Evaluation takes several guises. Funders often require formal program evaluation. To meet these requirements, partners collect data for each of their clients on indicators of school success, such as grades (23%), school attendance (31%, most frequently mentioned by the survey respondents), credit accumulation (26%), teacher evaluation (6%), graduation or attainment of the GED (10%), and enrollment in postsecondary education (16%). Other benchmarks relevant to meeting program goals include clients' worksite placement (6%) and employer evaluation (10%). Programs also collect data on clients' improvement on standardized tests and other measures: reading, language arts, and math scores; standard measures of early childhood development; and measurement of adult literacy, oral English, and parenting skills.

When funders request data other than that routinely compiled by schools, data collection can be problematic for the partnerships. For example, a family center had trouble collecting client contact data because it did not have staff to keep a contact log. Moreover, categories assumed by the funder were not meaningful because the center's programs blur distinctions between the served and server. The center negotiated a new data collection plan with the funder: going door-to-door in the community to ask people if they had used the center's services and, if so, for what purpose. The data collected in this way turned out to be not only satisfactory for the funder but also extremely useful in informing the center about how the community perceived it, who had received what services and resources, and what they might do to meet client needs more effectively. In the end, both the funder and the partnership were satisfied with this data collection activity.

Other programs are frustrated by external evaluations that do not report evaluation results to them, do not discuss the results with them, or do not tailor the evaluation to the program's needs. A staff member at one of the Miami alternative schools complained that these schools are evaluated in the same way as other schools. Although the results tend to be positive, they are not as useful as they could be if the unique features of the program were taken into account. Results from these external evaluations assure the school district that the schools are working, but they do not tell program directors what they want to know.

Programs also evaluate progress toward their goals by keeping track informally of program effects on individuals. In most cases, there is frequent communication among the partners and program staff members who are closest to the work. This occurs in the form of regular meetings and informal contact. Anecdotes reported in these contacts contribute to modifying programs incrementally.

Another aspect of informal evaluation is the proliferation of stories that capture high points in a program's life. Beyond improving grades and test scores and other indicators of the program's overall effectiveness, each program has stories about its effects on people. These compelling stories fortify the staff members and keep them focused. They serve as emblems of the program's concern with improving people's lives. The story of former gang members serving as staff members in the Filipino Youth Empowerment Program is one of these. At another site, a staff member described a storytelling instance during a funder's visit. When a program client cried while telling how the program had rescued her and her children, the visitor began to cry as well. Funding was renewed.

Although the school–CBO partnerships do engage in evaluation, this is the area about which there is the least confidence. Their forte is programs. They understand that evaluation is crucial both for keeping their programs on target and for justifying their work to those who want to know. Whether they are foundations, government agencies, or school districts, funders want evidence of impact. There is a need for new ways for school–CBO partnerships to gather objective data and keep comprehensive descriptive accounts. Another need is for ways to track programs' long-term effects on their clients.

In sum, programs considered by others in the field to be effective exhibit certain basic characteristics—adequate resources, structural and programmatic flexibility, responsive program design, and program evaluation. These characteristics of effective programs may be useful to others who are designing and operating new partnerships and programs if they are regarded as touchstones for development.

DISCUSSION

Beyond the basic descriptions of what partnerships do, how they work, and what characterizes successful partnerships, this study offers two general lessons. They concern the purpose of school–CBO partnerships' work with language minority students who may be at risk for school failure, and the need for more research.

Intense pressure on schools to improve test scores gives privilege to activities that have direct impact on academic achievement. Schools' resources are finite, and their traditions are firm: As they are currently configured, schools cannot take on all of the work that is essential to supporting academic achievement. Students who do not have that support must find it elsewhere or flounder. School partnerships with CBOs and other organizations help to broaden the base of support that language minority students are likely to need. Partnerships support academic achievement not by "mimicking schools" (C. Collier, personal communication, November 19, 1998), but by filling in and reinforcing the supports that schools have presumed in the past. Broadly viewed, they focus on helping students achieve school success, a construct composed of behaviors such as understanding and participating in instruction, attending school regularly, taking leadership in the school and community, and others. Supporting school success might require tutoring in the student's first language or it might require services that have traditionally been viewed as secondary to academic achievement—health care and advice on pregnancy prevention so that students can come to school, and parent education programs so that parents can help students with schoolwork. The partnerships understand that these services are not secondary at all. Rather, they are part of the base that students need to achieve academically. By sharing in this broader view that the partnerships take, schools can move toward more successfully retaining and educating language minority students who are at risk.

Much more needs to be known about the contributions of program staff members who share the clients' backgrounds and who have succeeded in moving into the social mainstream. This is an educational resource and a use of human capital that is very promising. Immigrants may be uniquely qualified to help schools and communities connect in supporting language minority students. They can make significant contributions in school–CBO partnerships, where staff certification is not an issue as it is in schools. They have an authority in this domain that allows them to guide and influence students at least as much as school personnel do. This phenomenon needs to be documented.

Finally, the fluid nature of successful school–CBO partnerships needs to be better understood. Their flexibility complements the well-documented rigidity (Darling-Hammond, 1997) of schools that contributes to their difficulties in serving at-risk language minority students. Documentation of how these two dynamics coexist or affect each other over time would be instructive.

ACKNOWLEDGMENTS

This work was supported under the Education Research and Development Program, PR/Award R306A60001, the Center for Research on Education, Diversity and Excellence, as administered by the Office of Educational Research and Improvement (OERI), National Institute on the Education of At-Risk Students (NIEARS), and the U.S. Department of Education (USDOE).

The contents, finding, and opinions expressed in this article are those of the author and do not necessarily represent the positions or policies of OERI, NIEARS, or the USDOE.

REFERENCES

Darling-Hammond, L. (1997). *The right to learn.* San Francisco: Jossey-Bass.

Davis, D. (1991). Adult literacy programs: Toward equality or maintaining the status quo? *Journal of Reading, 35,* 34–37.

Dryfoos, J. (1994a). Schools as places for health, mental health, and social services. In R. Takanishi (Ed.), *Adolescence in the 1990s* (pp. 82–109). New York: Teachers College Press.

Dryfoos, J. (1994b). Under one roof. *The American School Board Journal, 181,* 28–31.

Dryfoos, J. (1998). *Safe passage: Making it through adolescence in a risky society.* New York: Oxford University Press.

Erickson, F. (1986). Qualitative methods in research on teaching. In M. C. Wittrock (Ed.), *Handbook of research on teaching* (3rd ed., pp. 119–161). New York: Macmillan.

Heath, S. (1993). Inner city life through drama: Imagining the language classroom. *TESOL Quarterly, 27,* 177–192.

Heath, S., & McLaughlin, M. W. (1987). A child resource policy: Moving beyond dependence on school and family. *Phi Delta Kappan, 68,* 576–580.

Heath, S., & McLaughlin, M. W. (1991). Community organizations as family. *Phi Delta Kappan, 72,* 623–627.

Jones, B. (1992). Collaboration: The case for indigenous community-based organization support of dropout prevention programming and implementation. *Journal of Negro Education, 61,* 496–508.

Kirst, M. (1991). Improving children's services. *Phi Delta Kappan, 72,* 615–618.

National Coalition of Advocates for Students. (1994). *Delivering on promise: Positive practices for immigrant students.* Boston: Author.

Perrone, V. (1993). Learning for life: When do we begin? *Equity and Excellence in Education, 26,* 5–8.

Price, R., Gioci, M., Penner, W., & Trautlein, B. (1993). Webs of influence: School and community programs that enhance adolescent health and education. In R. Takanishi (Ed.), *Adolescence in the 1990s* (pp. 29–63). New York: Teachers College Press.

Roth, J., & Hendrickson, J. (1991). Schools and youth organizations. *Phi Delta Kappan, 72,* 619–622.

Rutherford, B., & Billig, S. (1995). Eight lessons of parent, family, and community involvement in the middle grades. *Phi Delta Kappan, 77,* 64–68.

Seeley, D. (1984). Educational partnership and the dilemmas of school reform. *Phi Delta Kappan, 65,* 383–388.

JOURNAL OF EDUCATION FOR STUDENTS PLACED AT RISK, 6(1&2), 27–44
Copyright © 2001, Lawrence Erlbaum Associates, Inc.

Finding Ways In: Community-Based Perspectives on Southeast Asian Family Involvement With Schools in a New England State

Francine F. Collignon, Makna Men, and Serei Tan

The Education Alliance
Brown University

In this article, we describe the barriers that Cambodian, Laotian, Hmong, and Vietnamese families in a New England state confront in participating in their children's education. We examine the resources from productive activities with community-based organizations (CBOs) that help them find ways to do so. CBO activities help families move beyond assumptions about education based on their experiences in their homelands to understanding schools in a new land. This article describes interactions linking students, their families, and communities. This article includes data obtained from (a) focus groups with 60 Southeast Asian community members who identify barriers to participating in the U.S. school system that their families confront; (b) writings from 4 participants of a Career Ladder Program who reflect on issues based on their own educational experiences; and (c) a Summer Academy for 85 Southeast Asian middle school students. Sociocultural theory frames the analysis of data. CBO–school relations that engage multiple partners in sustainable education initiatives result in gains for students and their families at the community, interpersonal, and personal levels.

During the last quarter of the 20th century, Cambodian, Laotian, Hmong, and Vietnamese families fled their homelands to escape hunger, torture, and violent death consequent to the Vietnam War. They created routes to freedom through jungles and land mines, across rivers and seas. Currently resettled in a New England state directly from Southeast Asia or via refugee camps elsewhere, these

---

Requests for reprints should be sent to Francine F. Collignon, The Education Alliance, Brown University, 222 Richmond Street, Suite 300, Providence, RI 02903–4226. E-mail: Francine_Collignon@brown.edu

families encounter another arduous journey: finding a way into the education system in the United States. The purpose of this article is to tell the story of their struggles to understand schools in a new land and to support their children's academic achievement.

This article examines Southeast Asian family involvement and participation in schools as part of our research at an institution of higher education joined with The Center for Research on Education, Diversity, and Excellence (CREDE). During the past 4 years, we have worked in varying degrees of collaboration with a community-based organization (CBO) that partners with a school district. This article reports findings of Year 3 of the research. To foreground Southeast Asian cultural perspectives, we have chosen to study the role of CBO–school relations primarily through the lens of community members.

We address two closely linked research questions: (a) What factors in the multiple cultures of Southeast Asian students—including the home, school, and community (in this study, ethnic associations and organizations)—promote or prevent their achievement of high standards? (b) How can school-based and community-based programs collaborate to achieve this goal? We argue that family and community involvement is a major factor in promoting student achievement. We believe that CBOs, especially those comprised of students' families and members of their ethnic communities, are uniquely positioned to take a lead in brokering relationships between the home and school.

To highlight this potential role for CBOs, we focus on the first of five principles advocated by CREDE for effective teaching and learning: to "facilitate learning through joint productive activity among teachers and students" (Tharp, 1997, p. 6). We apply this principle to our study of CBO–school relations, believing that "shared ways of understanding the world are created through the development of language systems and word meanings during shared activity" (Tharp, 1997, p. 6). This learning is demonstrated through our research project staff and a CBO directed and staffed by Southeast Asians providing technical assistance to one another and to schools. These collaborative activities have engaged Southeast Asian community members in (a) community focus groups in which 60 parents and family members participated, (b) a Career Ladder Program for 15 prospective teachers from the Southeast Asian communities, and (c) a Summer Academy for 85 Southeast Asian middle school students coordinated by the CBO with which we work.

Sociocultural theory frames our research study. Our activities with the CBO involve three levels of interactions (Rogoff, 1995). These levels, and the activities associated with them, include the community level (focus groups), the interpersonal level (a federally funded project for preservice and inservice teachers and their mentors), and the intrapersonal level (a Summer Academy for youth and their families). This study demonstrates the capacity of this Southeast Asian CBO, already in an informally constructed, ongoing relation with a school district, to lead multiple partnerships in breaking down barriers between home and school.

This article begins by presenting a sociohistorical background of the target population and highlights critical differences between education in these families' homelands and their new land. We then present key findings from community focus groups, from essays of participants in the Career Ladder Program, and from field notes from the youth Summer Academy. Finally, we illustrate how the value-added dimensions from the contributions of community-based initiatives, together with resources from schools, support family involvement and enhance student achievement through participation at the community, interpersonal, and intrapersonal levels.

SOCIOHISTORICAL BACKGROUND

The Cambodian, Laotian, Hmong, and Vietnamese families in this study began arriving in substantial numbers in the United States as a result of U.S. foreign policy in Southeast Asia and the political refugee status given to designated populations after the fall of Saigon (Karnow, 1983). The climate and urban neighborhoods where they resettled seemed ill suited for newcomers who had lived in milder climates and included farmers and seminomadic hill-tribe people as well as urban populations. The long-standing infrastructure in the state for settling refugees and immigrants, however, determined the site (Catlin & Beck, 1981). These refugee families came to the state in which we work because local groups or individuals working with voluntary agencies performing refugee resettlement expressed willingness to sponsor them (Lind, 1989). The agencies sponsoring refugees in the state recognized that multifamily housing could accommodate extended families and that jobs in the jewelry industry could employ populations with little or no proficiency in English. Still, the unfamiliar cultural practices and languages of the newcomers challenged the capacity of employers as well as service providers and educators (Governor's Council on Mental Health, Subcommittee on Refugee Services, 1988; Velazco, 1999).

Despite the fact that these are populations with four distinct languages and cultures, the Cambodian, Laotian, Hmong, and Vietnamese communities that comprise the majority of Southeast Asians in the state are lumped together within the census category of Asian-Pacific Islander in most demographic reports. Their numbers have fluctuated since 1975. These populations are part of more than 1 million refugee admissions to the United States from Southeast Asia between 1975 and 1998 according to data from Immigration and Refugee Services of America (Velazco, 1999). They also constitute about half of all political migrants permanently resettled in the Western world between 1975 and 1990 (Hein, 1995).

Although exact numbers are not available locally, CBOs and departments of state government servicing the four communities report the following current approximations: There are 18,000 to 20,000 Southeast Asians in the state, including

10,000 Cambodians, 3,000 Laotians, 3,000 Hmong, and 2,000 Vietnamese (Men, 2000). Approximately 80% of the Southeast Asian students in the state attend school in one school district, representing 10% of its student population. However, education information such as graduation, retention, dropout, or truancy rates are not disaggregated by membership in the four ethnic groups.

CBO: The Coalition

The CBO with which we collaborate has administered programs to address gaps in education, health, and social services since 1992. The CBO is a coalition of four mutual assistance associations (MAAs) that were funded by the state during the 1980s to help each of the four ethnic communities assist refugees from their own homeland. When it became clear that funding for MAAs was shrinking, the community leaders of the four MAAs formed a coalition intended to prevent duplicating services and to expand resources. A grant writer who was employed by one of the MAAs directed the start-up of the CBO (Lind, 1989) and soon transferred leadership to a Southeast Asian director.

Although these four ethnic communities did not share the same language and cultures and were not necessarily allies in their homelands, they joined forces and, in doing so, established a strong position for gaining support for services to their communities. In addition to participating in the new coalition, the four former MAAs maintained various ethnic organizations for their own members, primarily for cultural preservation and social exchange. The four distinct languages and cultures of these ethnic communities within the coalition presented challenges to their acting together as one organization in, for example, advocating for their children in schools. Over time, however, these four distinct ethnic groups have continued to work together through the CBO for the good of the communities. As of this writing, there are a minimum of five ongoing Southeast Asian CBOs, the coalition, and at least one group serving each ethnicity. In this article, the CBO to which we refer is the new coalition.

Changing Contexts for Education

Access to education is a challenge for any refugee population and its leaders. Finding ways into the culture of U.S. schools also has confounded these Southeast Asian families. These four communities brought with them beliefs and cultural practices with respect to teaching and learning that differed from one another and from prevalent beliefs and practices in the United States. Prior to their resettlement to New England in the mid-1970s, relatively few people from their homelands had lived in New England or attended its schools. Given that

there were no predecessors from their communities to orient the new populations to schools in a new country, understanding the local school districts was a
complex process for Southeast Asian populations.

The origins of formal schooling vary for the Cambodian, Laotian, Hmong, and
Vietnamese refugees depending on the sociohistorical influences in their home
countries. In the case of the Hmong of Laos, there was in fact no formal schooling
in their villages or written language until the 1950s (Yang, 1981). Traditional
schools in Cambodia were originally intended for learning the Cambodian language, writing, and Buddhist doctrine (Chhim, 1989), as were the temple schools
in Laos (Weinberg, 1997). Vietnamese schools were modeled after French schools
(Thuy, 1976). For the Hmong of Laos, learning was embedded in shared cultural
practices with adult community members in their hill-tribe villages rather than in
schools.

Repeated wars, political instability, and the introduction of foreign ideologies
influenced education in the homelands of these four Southeast Asian populations.
The dominant role of the teacher in the classroom, which allowed little participation from students and emphasized memorization and repetition, characterized the
Vietnamese system (Thuy, 1976), as well as the systems in Cambodia and Laos.
Although the Hmong in the United States come from Laos, their culture is vastly
different from that of Laotians. With its emphasis on repetition and memorization,
Hmong education—even with its lack of formal schools with classrooms—was
similar in this sense to Vietnamese education. Hmong "learned orally from their
parents or from the wise men in the village" (Yang, 1981, p. 9). They were taught
to respect the authority of the adult who was teaching them. They learned their traditional sung poetry, religious incantations, and instrumental music and memo-
rized the techniques of their textile art through repetition. "Repetition was a way of
life for the Hmong" (Collignon, 1994, p. 341).

War necessitated Southeast Asian families' flights to freedom and interrupted
their learning, because the fight to survive consumed every human resource. For
those families remaining in war-torn homelands, formal schooling came to a halt.
Eventually, in Cambodia there were no classrooms, students, teachers, or govern-
ment-level education departments. Textbooks of all types were burned. Students
in higher grades were condemned to die with their teachers (Chhim, 1989). According to informal interviews with members of the four Southeast Asian communities, families to varying degrees lost their capacity to continue formal schooling
or activities in their cities and villages because of war.

Many of the children whose learning opportunities were interrupted by atroci-
ties in their homelands during the Vietnam War and in the course of escape are
now the parents of children in U.S. schools. These parents do not understand the issues in U.S. schools, which differ dramatically from their own past educational experiences. Issues such as the changing expectations about the responsibilities and
roles of parents and teachers, discipline at school and at home, and new classroom

practices are sources of confusion today for Southeast Asian families (Tan, 1999). Traditionally, parents believed they had full responsibility for children at home, and teachers or adults in authority had full responsibility for children at school or in other learning settings. Parents and teachers in U.S. schools, however, expect help from each other and mutual involvement in their respective domains of home and school. The climate of U.S. schools is not severe and harsh, as families remember it to have been in their homelands. Best practices, such as cooperative learning and hands-on approaches, look like play instead of the hard work of learning to Southeast Asian parents (Tan, 1999). Classroom interactions, with teachers as participants, differ from the more formal teacher–learner relationships many of the Southeast Asian families knew in their past.

Family–School Partnerships

For members of the Southeast Asian communities, family involvement with schools is a new concept. Family involvement has roots in late 19th- and early 20th-century parent participation movements in the United States (Harry, 1992). Current frameworks for supporting family involvement (Epstein, 1995) are based on evidence that parental involvement with children's academics at home supports their achievement at school. Corresponding benefits can also come from families' funds of knowledge becoming accessible to schools (Moll, Amanti, Neff, & Gonzalez, 1992). How to provide these optimal conditions for students' academic progress remains a challenge for many immigrant and refugee families.

Sociocultural theory supports this study, which seeks to assist these families in supporting their children's lives at school. As was noted by August and Hakuta (1997),

> Enough research has been done on cultural differences in home socialization practices with regard to school learning that we know these differences exist. We have, however, almost no information about these issues for many of the ethnic groups that are now well represented among America's language-minority children. (p. 103)

Our research is an attempt to elicit this information from these populations, especially the attitudes toward involvement in their children's schools that they have based on socialization in their countries of origin.

Vygotsky believed in experiments that "make visible processes that are ordinarily hidden beneath the surface of habitual behavior" (Cole & Scribner, 1978, pp. 11–12). The search for these processes formed the basis for our initial collaboration with the CBO and our focus on its Summer Academy as an activity setting (Tharp & Gallimore, 1988). We set out as participant-observers to discover the hidden processes embedded in families' and community members' cultural constructions of an educational setting. The Summer Academy for Southeast Asian youth met the criteria outlined by Tharp and Gallimore (1988) that an activity setting be a context in which collaboration, interaction, intersubjectivity, assisted performance, and teaching occur. The Academy also provided a unit of analysis in which to study "interlocked dimensions" (Tharp & Gallimore, 1988) of home, community, and school. The focus groups and the Career Ladder Program we describe also emerged in part from the collaborations nurtured in the activity setting. In this study, we explore the resources brought to these activities by CBO–school partnerships. We believe that the partnerships bring value-added dimensions to otherwise separate interactions in the multiple cultures of students (Garcia, 1994).

METHOD

In the Southeast Asian Community Research Project, a four-member project staff from the Education Alliance at Brown University, including two Cambodian refugees, joined with the CBO by providing technical assistance and documenting detailed observations of CBO activities. We also held meetings to analyze and synthesize data. As representatives of higher education, our staff's participation expanded the CBO–school partnership to include still another partnership—that with the university. The collaborative activities in which we engaged were beneficial to the CBO, the school district, and the research designed to identify the ways that CBOs assist Southeast Asian families in supporting their children's education.

This article reports on work accomplished through collaboration with the CBO by providing technical assistance on issues affecting the education of its members' children. The technical assistance we report in this article includes the following components: (a) moderating a community meeting during which four focus groups were formed, assisting with the analysis of data, and developing a meeting agenda; (b) addressing the underrepresentation of Southeast Asian teachers in the school district by identifying a pool of prospective teachers from the Southeast Asian communities, assessing data, and assisting with the activities of a Career Ladder Program; and (c) acting as participant-observers and consultants to the youth Summer Academy.

Community Focus Groups

The CBO brought together Southeast Asian community members to provide their perspectives on the qualities they felt were necessary for leaders in their children's education, specifically the desired qualities for a new school district superintendent. These focus groups were established at the request of the chairperson of the search committee for a new superintendent in the local school district. The chairperson was also the president of the higher education institution where this research took place. The CBO enlisted our project staff's technical assistance in moderating the event. The planners of the group followed certain protocols, such as communicating through the CBO to act in collaboration with the leaders of the individual ethnic communities.

Announcements of the focus group meetings, translated into each different language, were sent out to community members. Notices were posted at Southeast Asian grocery stores and restaurants. Except for telephone calls and word of mouth, this was the only means of informing the community. The meeting took place at a high school on a Saturday morning. Sixty community members attended to voice their concerns about their children's education and their disappointment in having been excluded from membership on the search committee itself.

A brief introductory welcome and announcements for the entire group were translated into the four languages of the attending participants. Following the initial part of the meeting, the group divided according to language. The language facilitators for each language group, who were bilingual representatives from the Cambodian, Laotian, Hmong, and Vietnamese communities, conducted the focus group in their own native language. One person recorded the discussion in each group and reported back to the entire group. A question-and-answer session took place in the whole-group setting before the meeting adjourned. Interpreters were available in the large group when requested. The responses to detailed questions, recorded during participants' verbal exchanges, provided a window into the similar concerns they shared. This technique gave the meeting leader awareness of concerns not accessible through written surveys or by posing questions in participants' second languages. Subsequently, our staff met with community leaders to analyze the data and prepare a document that outlined parents' desired qualities of leadership and their concerns to be presented at a meeting with the chair of the search committee for the district superintendent.

Career Ladder for Southeast Asian Teachers

We began the Career Ladder project by assessing demographic data within the state with respect to Southeast Asian populations. We conducted a telephone poll of the 35 school districts in the state to determine the number of Southeast Asian students in each school district and, at the same time, to locate Southeast Asian teachers from those districts to assist with our research. Among the other findings that emerged, analysis of the data indicated the underrepresentation of Southeast Asian staff in schools in the state. From informal conversations with the CBO staff, personnel from local school districts, and Southeast Asian community members, we determined that there were community members interested in careers in teaching. We worked with the CBO staff to identify the multiple barriers preventing prospective teachers from proceeding on that career path.

As a result of the field notes from these conversations, and with the support of the CBO, school district, and state officials, our university applied for and was awarded federal funding to address the absence of teaching staff from the Southeast Asian communities by providing assistance in overcoming the identified barriers. The CBO, school district, and our project staff worked together to publicize the Career Ladder Program and recruit participants. Sixty-four Southeast Asian applicants sought to fill 15 openings and receive assistance in pursuing careers in teaching.

In this article, we report excerpts from autobiographical writing taken from course assignments that 4 Southeast Asian Career Ladder participants (2 preservice teachers and 2 inservice educators participating as mentor teachers) completed. The personal experiences recounted in the writings illustrate issues affecting the educational experiences of bilingual, bicultural learners pursuing careers in teaching. We were interested in spontaneous autobiography and in "how people go about telling their lives in their own ways" (Bruner, 1990, p. 122).

Summer Academy

Our research team has provided the CBO with consultation and professional development to assist with a Southeast Asian Summer Academy it has coordinated for the past 7 years. We perform a behind-the-scenes role. In collaboration with several other partners, we work with the CBO in implementing the activities of the summer school. We have participated in the formal opening and closing ceremonies. On a weekly basis, we have conducted participant observation in academic classes in English and math and recreational activities during the 8-week Academy. Descriptive analysis of data collected from detailed observations and interviews informs the project. These notes were reviewed by research team members and by multiple observers. Recurring themes are reported in the section to follow.

RESULTS

Themes

Three overriding themes emerged from the three activities in which we engaged with community members; namely, the community focus groups, the Career Ladder Program, and the Summer Academy. Evidence points to (a) insufficient knowledge of the educational system in the United States among Southeast Asian community members; (b) a lack of attention to issues of language proficiency and cultural competency in service provision to members of the Southeast Asian communities; and (c) low expectations of the Southeast Asian community members.

Community Focus Groups

In four focus groups, the Southeast Asian community members identified barriers to their involvement in their children's schools and determined what they needed to penetrate the barriers. The first barrier was insufficient knowledge about the school system among families and the community. They sought more information about who was responsible for different areas in the school district. They wanted a better understanding of how leaders, such as superintendents, were selected, what the rules were, and how they were enforced. A second barrier involved inadequate attention to language and cultural differences in schools. Participants wanted school staff members to understand the importance of the fact that all four Southeast Asian languages were not understood by all Southeast Asian students. They also needed translation and interpreter services at parent sessions and insisted on interpreter capacity in each school on a daily basis to deal with both routine and emergency communication with parents and families.

Participants also were concerned about the absence of personnel from their communities in all positions in schools, and desired resources to assist them in preparing for professional roles in their children's schools. Next, the participants were concerned that they were given no say in their children's education. Specifically, they wanted to address their children's truancy immediately, before it was too late. They needed all four Southeast Asian groups to work together to strengthen their position. They insisted on the importance of having a superintendent who had the capacity to understand Southeast Asian cultures.

Gaining an understanding of these cultures would enable school personnel to address—together with Southeast Asian parents—concepts new to them such as parent involvement and what it means in terms of the expectations held for families. In an informal interview, a community member asked

> What kind of involvement do teachers expect? There is confusion. Am I supposed to be a teacher, an advisor, a mentor, a coach, or a role model? I do not want to ask what "involvement" means at a meeting and "lose face."

An overriding concern among community members was that their noninvolvement in schools was perceived by others as not caring or having no interest in their children's education.

Career Ladder Program

In the Career Ladder Program, several collaborators meet regularly with a Learning Support Group for Southeast Asian inservice and preservice teachers. At an initial meeting, the teachers themselves requested that they meet regularly, approximately every 6 to 8 weeks. They listed topics of interest to them such as interviewing strategies and assistance with building professional portfolios. In addition, they suggested that workshops and courses in which they were enrolled together would enable them to get to know one another and support their professional growth.

Excerpts from the autobiographical essays of community members who participated in a course for Southeast Asian preservice and inservice teachers associated with the Career Ladder Program concurred with the educational needs addressed in the community focus groups. Similar to the challenges disclosed in the focus groups, these teachers recounted their own struggles to understand schools as newly arrived refugee students. The issues that emerged from their writing with respect to their own schooling indicate their growing awareness of the low expectations the school system held for them.

Excerpts from this first generation of Southeast Asian teachers in the United States follow. A woman from Laos wrote,

> At 12 years old I began my first day in an American school. I was lost in class because I had no idea of what was going on and didn't speak English. Being scared and confused and not able to communicate with others, I did not like this first day of my education.

This account illustrates the dilemma that the writer encountered when she entered a U.S. classroom for the first time as a student with no prior orientation to schools in the new land for either herself or her parents. No support had been provided to assist her in learning a second language, and no attention was given to cultural issues affecting her entry into the school. Recalling her introduction to secondary school, a Vietnamese woman wrote,

> During my first high school year, I was placed in the Special Education program because of lack of English. A year later, I managed to improve my English and was placed in the regular classes with the rest of the students.

A woman from Cambodia recalled, "The most difficult stage for me was the transition between two cultures. Growing up in an Asian culture, the family comes first and personal considerations second." Finally, and extending the discussion of these participants' struggles as students to those they faced as preservice teachers, a Cambodian man wrote that he "could not get a job anywhere in the state, despite constant publicity in the local press about the shortage of minority teachers" (Men, 1999a, p. 9). These anecdotes were written as events in the past; however, the writers were "deciding what to make of the past narratively at the moment of telling" (Bruner, 1990, p. 122). In fact, there were indications that their own new awareness of the challenges they had faced in their earlier learning experiences would inform their future teaching practice. Their writings reveal the same themes that emerged from the focus groups: insufficient knowledge of the school system, a need for attention to linguistic and cultural barriers of students and their families, and the importance to students of teachers and adults with high expectations for their future success.

Summer Academy

For 7 years, the Summer Academy has addressed the thematic issues evident in the focus group participants' accounts and the writings from teachers from Southeast Asian communities. Its primary goal has been to promote the academic success of Southeast Asian middle school youth; however, the program goes beyond academics to include social and health services as well. The program also extends beyond the summer, providing after-school study groups at selected middle schools during the academic year facilitated by tutors from a university and staff members from another CBO. In addition to academic enrichment, students can complete makeup work for failing grades in math and English during the previous school year by participating in the Summer Academy. Their participation in the Academy also enables them to access ongoing assistance in its after-school component.

The number of middle school students from the Cambodian, Laotian, Hmong, and Vietnamese communities who attend the Academy varies from year to year depending on available funding. It has ranged from 45 to 90 students. The students are recruited by the CBO staff members from the school district. The staff members visit students' homes to explain the program's goals to students and their families, seek family support in ensuring attendance, and obtain parental permission. Although parents register their children and sign forms indicating their understanding of the guidelines for their children's participation, the number of students grows throughout the summer from walk-ins.

The Academy's opening event begins with the introduction of public officials from city and state governments and invited guests from neighboring CBOs and higher education institutions. Community leaders set the tone of high expectations for the participants. In their opening speeches, they praise participants for choosing to attend the Academy and link summer studies to helping students become good citizens. The speakers encourage parents to be proud of their children. The 8 weeks to come are described as serious and worthwhile. A corps of Southeast Asian staff from the CBO assist with the celebration and serve refreshments to students' families and guests from the community at large.

A typical day at the Academy combines academic work with social activities as incentives for participation. Classroom instruction is provided by native English speaking teachers to support the participants' English language proficiency. They also provide math instruction and physical education activities. Recreation includes a daily swim in the pool on a college campus and weekly field trips to historic sites in the state or to recreational destinations. CBO staff members chaperon field trips and tutor in classrooms. Parents and CBO staff members take daily attendance and immediately investigate any absences from the program. They visit absentees' homes and engage family members in determining truant students' whereabouts. Family members also become cultural consultants to the program. They provide background information and hands-on instruction in the arts, such as teaching dance, song, and storytelling, as well as demonstrations using cultural artifacts, traditional clothing from students' homelands, and food preparation.

In formal and informal interviews, parents and staff from the communities expressed their concerns about the students' safety, health issues, gang involvement, and boredom at home, all of which the program addresses. More than a traditional summer school for content-area remediation, this activity setting represents a co-constructed approach to engaging students in a learning community with personal, academic, and social rewards.

Despite its history in the community, the Summer Academy relies on "soft money," has no permanent site, and has been historically underfunded with respect to participants' needs. The school district in which the majority of its participants are enrolled has provided varying degrees of support, such as transportation, textbooks, curriculum materials, and sometimes space (by allowing use of a school facility). The Academy's teaching staff comprises certified educators who agree to align their instruction with the district's middle school curriculum. An ongoing relation exists between the CBO and the school district; however, it is not formalized in terms of commitments of ongoing support for the Summer Academy. Changes in personnel at either the CBO or the school can affect the relation.

CONCLUSION

It can be said that members of these Southeast Asian communities faced struggles in getting out of their war-ravaged countries that parallel those they now face in "getting in" the educational system of their new homeland. When the first refugees from Southeast Asia came to the Northeast in 1975, many opted for resettlement in any host country rather than face oppression or death in their homelands. Although uncertain of their final destination, they found ways to escape. These families' experiences with their children's education is another challenge, related in that it requires finding a route to overcome obstacles. The families in this study have a clear goal for their children to receive the highest quality education possible. The destination is now certain, but the route they must take to get there is not (Men, 1999b). The challenge is finding ways to get in.

As our description of the community focus group reveals, Southeast Asian populations continue to come together to find ways into decision-making processes about their children's education in a society many of them do not understand. They realize the importance of education for their children, but the focus group interactions demonstrate that they do not understand the school system itself. In fact, when asked to discuss the qualities they desired in a new superintendent, they did not know the meaning of the word *superintendent.*

For parents, unclear expectations and the inability to clarify their own roles with schools persist. Social factors, such as parents' lack of time at home because of jobs and family responsibilities, impede their ability to help with their children's homework and to spend time at their schools. Educational factors such as parents' absence of prior education, interrupted schooling, low proficiency level in the schools' language of instruction, and limited experience with the culture of U.S. schools make families' direct involvement difficult.

As we have reported, barriers to full participation of Southeast Asian students from Cambodia, Laos, and Vietnam; their families; and their communities in the culture of schools in an urban setting in a New England state are varied. Factors as apparent as language and as invisible as conflicting worldviews prevent their access to information and effective participation in activities. In the case of prospective teachers, understanding the complexities of the teacher preparation process, finding the resources to complete studies, and accessing networks to help them secure professional employment in schools is difficult.

Detailed observations at the Summer Academy through participant observation by research staff from both inside and outside of the Southeast Asian communities contribute to our perspectives. In our observations, we noted that students engaged in classroom instruction in the Summer Academy activities when they were "demonstrated rather than only explained" (Tan, 1999). The emphasis on repetition that parents expect because of their past educational experiences does not match their children's school experience. The struggles of parents and educators to align mutual expectations about their roles in children's education are intensified by their unfamiliarity with each other's languages and cultures. Students encounter intergenerational conflicts in the family when behaviors that are acceptable at school put them at odds with the traditional practices of their elders at home. These clashes intensify families' lack of understanding of schools and do nothing to provide answers to their questions about where and how families and members of their ethnic communities fit in.

Signs of Progress

Many barriers still block the way to full participation of Southeast Asian communities in the life of schools. As Tharp et al. (1999) put it, "Communities whose children are at greatest academic risk have found school reform slow in coming, difficult to achieve, and often contentious in process" (p. 6). The 25-year-long efforts of Southeast Asians to participate fully in schools in the state where we conducted this study reflect this slow pace of school reform. Some efforts to remove the barriers meet with contention. As of this writing, however, there are also signs of progress. These signs include the following:

1. A Southeast Asian Advisory Council made up of representatives from the leadership of the four communities meets regularly and engages in inquiry and discussion with the superintendent of the district where 80% of the target population lives.
2. Representatives from the communities serve as members of working committees in the school district, and the number of credentialed teachers in classrooms from the Southeast Asian communities is growing.
3. At least 30 prospective Southeast Asian teachers engage in course work and practica, preparing for careers in teaching.
4. The school district in the state with the most Southeast Asian families includes a component to build "Family and Community Partnerships" in the new district plan.
5. The Summer Academy continues with the largest number of students in its 8-year history.

Examples from our collaborations also provide signs of progress and demonstrate CREDE's principle of engaging in joint productive activity (Tharp, 1997). By engaging in collaborative activities with the CBO, we and its multiple other partners—the city, state, and institutions of higher education—teach and learn from each other. This mediated learning has been accomplished by (a) learning from actions we took together to convene community members in focus groups about their concerns for education, (b) helping recruit and support a first generation of teachers from four Southeast Asian communities, and (c) joining in multiple partnerships and providing technical assistance to support youth in a framework broader than academics through the Summer Academy. The community meeting, the efforts to support new teachers from the Southeast Asian community, and the structure and content of the Summer Academy demonstrate the three levels of interaction within a sociocultural construct led by a CBO.

Implications of the Research

Engaging in mutually productive activity requires communication to determine appropriate starting points. Assumptions must be examined. In our research, we found that the community members in the focus groups needed to gain a clearer understanding of the school system before addressing the qualities they desired in a new superintendent. Prospective teachers needed to address barriers they faced in their own education before proceeding with a career plan. Groups collaborating to provide quality educational experiences for youth need to assess the needs and available resources within the multiple partnerships.

We are convinced that CBOs and individual schools or school districts can develop partnerships and proceed effectively by engaging in a series of mutually beneficial productive activities. Through these activities, issues of infrastructure can be anticipated and planned for. If the family involvement agenda is given priority in these collaborations, schools and parents can clarify mutual expectations about education through their work together. Although CBOs and other organizations of their nature often struggle to maintain the infrastructure, leadership skills, and resources necessary for sustainability (Adger, 2001/this issue), we believe schools, districts, and universities have sustained resources that CBOs do not.

At a time when a "one size fits all" climate prevails in education, we believe that engagement with CBO–school relations provides an effective alternative. Our research suggests that there is the potential for any successful CBO–school relation to play a role in closing the distance between the multiple worlds (Azmitia & Cooper, 2001/this issue) through which students navigate. Family involvement takes a new shape when it is led and sustained by CBO–school relations.

ACKNOWLEDGMENTS

This work was supported under the Education Research and Development Program, PR/Award R306A60001, the Center for Research on Education, Diversity and Excellence, as administered by the Office of Educational Research and Improvement (OERI), National Institute on the Education of At-Risk Students (NIEARS), and the U.S. Department of Education (USDOE).

The contents, finding, and opinions expressed in this article are those of the authors and do not necessarily represent the positions or policies of OERI, NIEARS, or the USDOE.

We appreciate the ongoing support and encouragement for our research from colleagues at The Education Alliance at Brown University, especially from Adeline Becker, Maria Pacheco, Deborah Collins, and Edmund Hamann. We acknowledge our collaboration with Cambodian, Laotian, Hmong, and Vietnamese community members, with special thanks to Joseph Le. We are also grateful for the contributions to our thinking and for critical commentary from Amanda Datnow, Catherine Cooper, Patricia Gandara, and Tiffany Meyers, who assisted us in the completion of the article.

REFERENCES

Adger, C. T. (2001/this issue). School–community-based organization partnerships for language minority students' school success. *Journal of Education for Students Placed At Risk, 6.*

August, D., & Hakuta, K. (Eds.). (1997). *Improving schooling for language minority children: A research agenda.* Washington, DC: National Academy Press.

Azmitia, M., & Cooper, C. (2001/this issue). Good or bad? Peer influences on Latino and European American adolescents' pathways through school. *Journal of Education for Students Placed At Risk, 6.*

Bruner, J. (1990). *Acts of meaning.* Cambridge, MA: Harvard University Press.

Catlin, A., & Beck, S. (1981). *The Hmong from Asia to Providence* (Rep. No. 0002). Providence, RI: Roger Williams Park Museum Publication.

Chhim, S. H. (1989). *Introduction to Cambodian culture.* San Diego, CA: San Diego State University, Multifunctional Resource Center.

Cole, M., & Scribner, S. (Eds.). (1978). *Mind in society: The development of higher psychological processes.* Cambridge, MA: Harvard University Press.

Collignon, F. F. (1994). From "paj ntaub" to paragraphs: Perspectives on Hmong processes of composing. In V. John-Steiner, C. F. Panofsky, & L. W. Smith (Eds.), *Sociocultural approaches to language and literacy: An interactionist perspective* (pp. 331–346). New York: Cambridge University Press.

Epstein, J. (1995). School/family/community partnerships: Caring for the children we share. *Phi Delta Kappan, 76,* 701–712.

Garcia, E. (1994). *Understanding and meeting the challenge of student cultural diversity.* Boston: Houghton Mifflin.

Governor's Council on Mental Health, Subcommittee on Refugee Services. (1988). *Meeting the mental health needs of Rhode Island's Southeast Asian communities.* Providence, RI: The Refugee Mental Health Planning Project.

Harry, B. (1992). *Cultural diversity, families, and the special education system: Communication and empowerment.* New York: Teachers College Press.

Hein, J. (1995). *From Vietnam, Laos, and Cambodia: A refugee experience in the United States.* New York: Twayne.

Karnow, S. (1983). *Vietnam: A history.* New York: Viking.

Lind, L. (1989). *The Southeast Asians in Rhode Island: The new Americans.* Providence: The Rhode Island Heritage Commission and the Rhode Island Publications Society.

Men, M. (1999a, Winter). Reflections on access. In *Equity News, A Publication of the New England Equity Assistance Center* (pp. 9, 11).

Men, M. (1999b). [Unpublished research materials]. Providence, RI: Brown University, The Education Alliance.

Men, M. (2000). [Unpublished research materials]. Providence, RI: Brown University, The Education Alliance.

Moll, L. C., Amanti, C., Neff, D., & Gonzalez, N. (1992). Funds of knowledge for teaching: Using a qualitative approach to connect homes and classrooms. *Theory Into Practice, 31*(2), 132–141.

Rogoff, B. (1995). Observing sociocultural activity on three planes: Participatory appropriation, guided participation, and apprenticeship. In J. V. Wertsch, P. del Rio, & A. Alvarez (Eds.), *Sociocultural studies of mind* (pp. 139–164). Cambridge, England: Cambridge University Press.

Tan, S. (1999). [Unpublished research materials]. Providence, RI: Brown University, The Education Alliance.

Tharp, R. G. (1997). *From at-risk to excellence: Research, theory, and principles for practice.* Santa Cruz: University of California, Santa Cruz, Center for Research on Education, Diversity, and Excellence.

Tharp, R. G., & Gallimore, R. (1988). *Rousing minds to life: Teaching, learning and schooling in social context.* New York: Cambridge University Press.

Tharp, R. G., Lewis, H., Hilberg, R., Bird, C., Epaloose, G., Dalton, S. S., Youpa, D. G., Rivera, H., Riding In-Feathers, M., & Eriacho, W., Sr. (1999). Seven more mountains and a map: Overcoming obstacles to reform in Native American schools. *Journal of Education for Students Placed At Risk, 4,* 5–25.

Thuy, V. G. (1976). *Getting to know the Vietnamese and their culture.* New York: Frederick Ungar.

Velazco, A. (1999, March). *Survival and adaptation in the refugee experience.* Paper presented at the TESOL Conference, New York.

Weinberg, M. (1997). *Asian-American education: Historical background and current realities.* Mahwah, NJ: Lawrence Erlbaum Associates, Inc.

Yang, S. K. (1981). The Hmong of Laos: 1896–1978. In *Refugee education guides: Glimpses of Hmong history and culture* (General Information Series, No. 16, pp. 3–17). Alexandria, VA: Center for Applied Linguistics.

JOURNAL OF EDUCATION FOR STUDENTS PLACED AT RISK, 6(1&2), 45–71
Copyright © 2001, Lawrence Erlbaum Associates, Inc.

Good or Bad? Peer Influences on Latino and European American Adolescents' Pathways Through School

Margarita Azmitia

Department of Psychology
University of California, Santa Cruz

Catherine R. Cooper

Department of Psychology and Department of Education
University of California, Santa Cruz

Drawing on Sociocultural and Bridging Multiple Worlds models, this article reports 2 longitudinal studies of peers as resources and challenges for students' school performance and future planning. Study 1 examined European American and Latino students' perceptions of peers' emotional support, academic guidance, and companionship from elementary to junior high school. In both school years, most students had at least 1 friend who provided each resource. Links between resources and grades were stronger in junior high than in elementary school. As predicted, students' perceptions of peers' overall encouragement or discouragement of school were linked to English and math grades. Study 2 examined peers as challenges and resources for youth in a community college academic outreach program. Participants saw peers as both challenges and resources in reaching career goals and as greater challenges than families. High school youth in 1 cohort saw peers as greater challenges than did younger youth. Reported peer challenges and resources were modestly related to math pathways. Taken together, the studies illustrate the significance of peers as both resources and challenges to adolescents as they navigate the crucial years that will determine their college eligibility and career options.

Requests for reprints should be sent to Margarita Azmitia or Catherine R. Cooper, Psychology Department, Social Sciences, II, University of California, Santa Cruz, CA 95064. E-mail: azmitia@cats.ucsc.edu and ccooper@cats.ucsc.edu

The often challenging transition from elementary school to middle or junior high school can shape students' long-term pathways in school and work. Many students, especially ethnic minorities and low-income youth, show declining school grades and expectations for their future. By high school, these students are overrepresented in remedial tracks and underrepresented in college-preparatory classes (Cooper, Jackson, Azmitia, & Lopez, 1998; Mehan, Villanueva, Hubbard, & Lintz, 1996). Identifying the resources as well as the challenges that these youth face is especially critical in California, where minority students will outnumber majority students in the coming decades (Larson & Rumberger, 1995).

Peers can play a pivotal role in both majority and minority students' school pathways through their joint participation in school activities as well as in decisions to stay in school and in developing college and career identities (Gándara, 1995; Romo & Falbo, 1996). This article reports two related longitudinal studies of students' perceptions of their peers as resources for and challenges to school and future planning. In the first study, we examined European American and Latino students' perceptions of their peers' emotional support, academic guidance (discussing the future and helping with homework), and companionship during the transition from elementary to junior high school. We also assessed students' views of whether, in general, their peers encouraged (i.e., were a resource) or discouraged (i.e., were a challenge) them to do well in school. In the second study, we examined the idea of peers as challenges and resources for youth participating in a setting where peers might play a positive role: a community college academic outreach program. One way such programs might help students stay in school and on track to college is by creating networks of friends who value school and have college identities (Mehan et al., 1996). For both studies, we drew on the two related perspectives of Sociocultural theory and the Bridging Multiple Worlds model to consider the roles of peers during the transition from childhood to adolescence.

SOCIOCULTURAL THEORY

Sociocultural approaches view children's participation in everyday cultural practices or activity settings, whether household chores, classroom cooperative learning projects, or soccer games, as the core of personal, interpersonal, and cultural or institutional development (Rogoff, 1998). Researchers have mapped these cultural practices in terms of who participates (e.g., children, parents, siblings, friends, or teachers), how communication occurs (e.g., silent demonstration, one-way oral instruction, or group conversations), and what values motivate members of cultural communities (whether social acceptance, attending college, or supporting one's family financially; for reviews see Greenfield & Cocking, 1994; Jacob & Jordan, 1993; Rogoff, 1998; Tharp & Gallimore, 1988).

Within the sociocultural perspective, schools that capitalize on students' knowledge, values, and practices beyond the classroom enhance students' school engagement and success (see Gonzalez, Andrade, Civil, & Moll, 2001/this issue; Moll & Whitmore, 1993). As students move through adolescence and spend more time in their communities and with peers, they participate in a growing range of activity settings and cultural practices. Like parents, siblings, relatives, teachers, and other adults, peers help students learn the practices of their schools and cultural communities (Eckert, 1989; Gándara, 1995). In Study 1, we explored peers' roles in two interpersonal practices, emotional support and companionship, and two academic practices, completing homework and discussing future educational and career goals. In Study 2, we investigated how peers function as both resources and challenges in the lives of youth from low-income families who were participating in a community college outreach program that provides opportunities for youth to work together on their goals for college and careers.

Although both studies examined students' perceptions of peer resources and challenges, Study 1 employed an *etic* approach, and Study 2, an *emic* approach. In Study 1 we assumed students would perceive their peers as resources for and challenges to school, and we tested hypotheses about three resources identified by researchers as key functions of relationships. We also assessed students' overall perceptions of peers' encouragement and discouragement of school with a standardized survey and explicit questions about peers. This etic or "outsider" perspective allowed us to align our study with research literature and debates about positive and negative roles of peers in students' school pathways, but it was not sensitive to youths' own meanings. In Study 2, we asked students to write about their resources and challenges with open-ended questions about who and what they saw as challenges and resources in achieving their educational and career goals. These emic, "insider" perspectives are valuable in testing our theories about youths' lives and experiences. By comparing results of the two studies, we could map similarities and differences from complementary quantitative and qualitative methods and enrich our understanding of linkages between peers and school achievement.

THE BRIDGING MULTIPLE WORLDS MODEL

This model, which is compatible with sociocultural theory, focuses on how youth learn to move across the contexts of their families, peers, schools, and communities, sometimes easily and sometimes with difficulty (Cooper, Cooper, Azmitia, Chavira, & Gullatt, in press). Its original formulation, known as the Students' Multiple Worlds Model, was proposed by educational anthropologists Phelan, Davidson, and Yu (1991) to learn how high school youth navigate across their family, peer, and school contexts. Phelan et al. chose the geographical metaphor of *world* to refer to the cultural knowledge and expectations held in each social context and *navigation* to capture youths' experiences as they try to move across borders between worlds.

The Bridging Multiple Worlds model extends the work of Phelan et al. (1991) in two ways. We added a major focus on community-based organizations (e.g., academic outreach programs, sports, and religious organizations) as worlds that can serve as bridges along students' pathways to college and adulthood. We also added a developmental focus to trace students' identity development and school achievement from childhood through college (Cooper et al., in press). In Study 1 we focused on students' navigation between their peer and school worlds during the transition from elementary to junior high school; in Study 2, we considered changes in students' academic pathways and experiences across their school, peer, and community program worlds as they moved from junior high to high school.

A CLOSER LOOK AT THE ROLE OF PEERS IN STUDENTS' ACADEMIC ACHIEVEMENT

Many studies document the positive role of peers in providing emotional support, academic guidance, and companionship as well as the role of these resources in motivation, adjustment, and achievement from elementary to junior high school (Berndt & Keefe, 1995; Eccles, 1999; Hymel, Comfort, Schonert-Reichl, & McDougall, 1996). However, other studies reveal few links between these resources and positive school outcomes. Hymel et al. (1996) suggested that not all students have friends who support school, so links between peer experiences and academic indicators may occur only among those students who do have such relationships.

Sociologists and educational anthropologists, however, have also shown that especially for minority and low-income students, peers can challenge students' achievement motivation and achievement and their pursuit of higher education (Delgado-Gaitán, 1986; Eckert, 1989; Fordham & Ogbu, 1986; Gibson, 1993; Hymel et al., 1996; Willis, 1977). Fordham and Ogbu (1986) and Willis (1977) suggested that for these youth, schools can re-create patterns of discrimination and racism that exist in the larger society. Joining other alienated peers, youths' development of oppositional identities reflects a reasonable response to unfair educational practices. That is, students come to believe that doing well in an institution that discriminates against them is tantamount to "selling out" and "acting White."

Although oppositional school identities characterize some students, the negative portrayal of minority and low-income students' peers cannot explain why some youth from ethnic minority and low-income groups succeed in school and why some ethnic majority, affluent youth fail. Brown (1990) addressed this question in his study of academic success and failure stories in an ethnically diverse high school. He found that, although most youth held positive attitudes toward school, some showed the oppositional patterns reported in other research. Rather than peers influencing students to develop positive or negative attitudes toward school, however, Brown found that it was youth themselves who chose to befriend peers with similar academic values. Over time, these friends reinforced one another's positive or negative school identities, thus contributing to their success or failure in school. Building on Brown's study of high school students, Study 1 assessed whether peer groups who support or discourage schooling are already evident in junior high school. Although we did not assess friendship formation (i.e., how students constituted their peer groups), the years from elementary to junior high school are marked by fluidity and change in friendships. Indeed, in analyses that were not part of this report we found that most of the students showed dramatic changes in their friendship circles.[1]

COMMUNITY PROGRAMS AS PATHWAYS TO ACADEMIC ACHIEVEMENT AND IDENTITY

The people and experiences students encounter in community programs can play key roles in helping them gain educational and career-related experiences, feel confident and safe in their neighborhoods, learn alternatives to violence, and find ways to navigate across their worlds of home, school, and community (Cooper, Denner, & Lopez, 1999). In ethnic minority communities, program staff members often come from and value children's home communities and often share a common language and sometimes a family history with the children. Staff members can pass on their understanding of how to retain ties to their cultural community while succeeding in mainstream schools. Programs also provide opportunities for youth to talk and write about their dreams for their future careers, education, and families. Research indicates such programs can play key roles in fostering future orientation and leadership as well as academic skills (see Adger, 2001/this issue).

College outreach programs, in particular, offer intergenerational resources for students to develop academic skills and academic and college identities. College student tutors provide tips for academic success and serve as role models, and program activities foster new friendships and networks of support for academic identities. Such support may or may not be available from peers from schools or neighborhoods. Outreach programs across the United States, such as Upward Bound, Early Academic Outreach Program (EAOP), Puente, Advancement Via Individual Determination (AVID), and Math, Engineering, Science Achievement

---

[1]An examination of students' school records indicated that, consistent with Brown's (1990) research, students associated with friends who were performing similarly in school. It is still the case, however, that these data do not allow us to determine whether this similarity motivated friendship formation or whether it evolved over time.

(MESA), have both unique and common elements and criteria for eligibility. They typically include family involvement, academic counseling, mentoring and tutoring, field trips to colleges and universities, test and application essay preparation, and career development activities. Program activities may take place during the school day or in Saturday or summer programs on college campuses. Gándara, Larson, Mehan, and Rumberger (1998) mapped how outreach programs foster change in individual students, families, schools, and partnerships in a variety of ways, including building social networks and academic identities.

In sum, the two longitudinal studies reported in this article assessed the role of peers in Latino and European American adolescents' school performance and opportunities to discuss their educational and career goals. In Study 1, we followed Latino and European American students from elementary school to junior high school to assess gender and ethnic variation in the association between positive and negative characteristics of their friends and peer group and their math and English grades. In Study 2, we assessed the role of peers among students in a program designed to promote college attendance in low-income youth to assess their perceptions of peers as challenges and resources, their school pathways, and the role of peers in these pathways.

STUDY 1

This study addressed four research questions:

1. Are there gender and ethnic differences in students' perceptions of the availability of friends for emotional support, academic guidance, and companionship during the transition from elementary to junior high school?
2. Is the availability of these peer resources associated with English and math grades during the transition from elementary to junior high school?
3. In junior high school, are there ethnic and gender differences in students' perceptions of peers' overall encouragement or discouragement of schooling?
4. What is the association between junior high school students' perceptions of peers' encouragement and discouragement of schooling and their English and math grades?

We focused on Math and English grades because they tap key domains in elementary and junior high school and play critical roles in tracking students into college-bound or vocational tracks (Henderson, 1997).

Numerous studies have shown that friends are important resources for students' emotional support, academic guidance, and companionship needs (for reviews, see Bukowski, Newcomb, & Hartup, 1996). Adolescents with friends who provide these resources perform better at school and have an easier time adjusting to junior high school than students whose friends do not serve these functions (Berndt & Keefe, 1995; Cauce, Mason, Gonzales, Hiraga, & Liu, 1996). Because research on the relation between these peer resources and academic achievement has focused primarily on European American students, our first goal was to explore potential gender and ethnic variation in the availability of these resources in elementary school and junior high school.

Based on previous studies, for our second question we predicted that students whose peers provided these resources would have higher math and English grades in elementary and junior high school than students whose peers did not serve these functions. Because access to friendships that provide emotional support, academic guidance, and companionship helps early adolescents adjust to the transition from elementary to junior high school, we also examined whether the relation between peer resources and English and math grades was stronger in junior high than in elementary school. That is, we predicted an interaction between students' year in school and the availability of these peer resources on school grades.

Our third question concerned students' perceptions of the overall positive and negative qualities of their peer networks for school; that is, whether they viewed their peers as resources for (i.e., encouraging) or challenges to (i.e., discouraging) academics. Asking youth about specific friends who provide emotional support, academic guidance, and companionship may lead them to focus on only positive friendships, but asking about overall encouragement and discouragement for school across students' peer networks may yield different results. In support of this view, research evidence of negative pressures of peers on schooling is based on asking youth about the overall properties of their peer networks. This approach may be more likely to reveal peer pressure to cut classes; drop out of school; or experiment with drugs, sex, alcohol, or shoplifting, which bears great costs for students' lives (Berndt, Laychak, & Park, 1990; Fordham & Ogbu, 1986). To test this possibility, when students were in junior high school, we asked them to rate their peers' overall support and discouragement of school. We expected to replicate prior research by finding that European American students reported more peer encouragement for school and Latino students reported more discouragement from peers. Based on reports by Fordham and Ogbu (1986) with African American youth and Romo and Falbo (1996) with Latino youth that low-income minority boys experience more academic discouragement from peers than girls do, we predicted Latino boys would report the most peer discouragement in our sample.

Finally, our fourth question assessed the relation between peers' encouragement and discouragement for schooling and students' grades. When parents and teachers try to understand students' declining motivation and grades in the first year of junior high school, they often assume peers play a significant role in their academic difficulties. However, peers' encouragement can also keep students motivated and on track to college. Thus, for some students, peers encourage schooling, whereas for others they challenge it. If peer encouragement promotes school success, students' perceptions of peer encouragement should be correlated with English and math grades. If peer challenges are also linked to achievement, students' perceptions of discouragement from peers should be negatively correlated with grades.

Method

Participants

The initial sample consisted of 113 Latino and European American early adolescent boys and girls participating in a larger longitudinal study (Azmitia & Cooper, 1996). Our study focused on these ethnic groups because they are the largest in our central California community. Seven students did not complete the study, leaving a final sample of 106. Attrition was similar across the four cells of the design. Thirty-eight students (19 boys and 19 girls) were Latino and 68 (35 girls and 33 boys) were European American. Mean age for both ethnic groups in Year 1 was 11.7 years. Seventy-nine percent of Latinos and 21% of European American students were low income, defined by eligibility for free or reduced-price lunches at school. This income distribution resembles the school district figures for the four schools (71% of low-income Latinos, 24% of low-income European American students).

Forty-seven percent of Latino students were born outside the United States, all but 2 in Mexico. Ninety-four percent of the Latino students had at least one parent born outside the United States, in all but 2 cases, in Mexico; for 85% of students, both parents were immigrants. The mean level of schooling for Latino fathers and mothers was ninth and eighth grade, respectively. Seventy-six percent of the Latino fathers and 59% of the Latino mothers were employed, typically in semiskilled and unskilled occupations (Hollingshead & Redlich, 1958). The mean number of years of schooling for European American fathers and mothers was 15 (many had college degrees). Ninety-four percent of fathers and 88% of mothers were employed, typically in professional and administrative positions, although some mothers worked in clerical or sales positions. The mean numbers of siblings for Latino and European students were 3.29 and 2.46, respectively.

The students were recruited from six sixth-grade classrooms in four elementary schools that, according to school district records, served a large number of Latino students and the highest proportion of low-income European American students in the district. We sought a large sample of low-income students whose achievement spanned a broad range. Letters in English and Spanish were sent to parents of all students in the six classrooms inviting them to participate in the 2-year study.[2] Parents who did not return the consent form within 2 weeks received follow-up phone

---

[2]This sampling method recruited a small number of students of African and Asian descent. Given their small numbers, their data were excluded from this article.

calls. These recruiting techniques yielded reasonably high levels of participation, ranging from 61% to 85% across the six classrooms, with an average of 74%.

Materials

As part of our larger study, students completed measures of their family, school, and peer contexts. For this article, we report those concerning peers and school achievement.

Peer resources.   Friends' provision of emotional support, academic guidance, and companionship was assessed with the Circle of Friends Interview (Azmitia, Cooper, Wishard, Thrush, & Ittel, 1998). Parts of this interview were adapted from Azmitia, Ittel, and Kamprath's (1997) Early Adolescence Friendship Interview. The first section of the Circle of Friends Interview assesses demographic characteristics (e.g., age, gender, ethnicity, academic achievement, whether the friend is a relative) of up to 15 friends in adolescents' friendship networks (up to 5 best friends, up to 5 close friends, and up to 5 just friends, typically acquaintances). Subsequent sections assess domains and intensity of peer pressure, the frequency with which adolescents engage in a range of positive (e.g., reading books, going to church, spending time with friends) and negative activities (e.g., skipping school, worrying about fitting in with friends, spending time with friends whom parents dislike), an inventory of people with whom adolescents discuss issues (e.g., problems, the future, and social events), and adolescents' assessment of their defining qualities.

For this article, we report only parts of the interview containing adolescents' friendship nominations (i.e., their circle of friends), friends from their circle with whom they spent time at school and outside of school, and perceptions of members of their circle who provided emotional support, academic guidance, and companionship. We also assessed resources from students' perceptions of friends' overall support for schooling. Friends' provision of emotional resources was assessed with the following three questions: Who do you talk to about problems at home? Who do you talk to about good things that happen to you at school? and Who do you talk to about bad things that happen to you at school? Academic guidance resources were assessed for long-term career planning (i.e., conversations about the future) and the more immediate goal of completing homework. Friends' guidance in planning the future was assessed by the question, Who do you talk to about the future, like how far you want to go in school, what job you want, or in general, about growing up? Friends' guidance with homework was assessed with the question, Who do you talk with to get help with homework? Friends' providing companionship was assessed with the following three questions: Which friends do you hang out with during your free time at school? Which of your friends do you hang out with outside of school? and Who do you talk to about social things, like friends, gossip, who you like, and social events?

Preliminary analyses revealed students varied in the number of friends in their circle and whether they had an extensive pattern of friendships (i.e., drew resources from many friends) or an intensive pattern (i.e., drew resources from one or a few friends). These individual differences did not appear to be systematically related to ethnicity, gender, or academic achievement. Thus we recoded the data to reflect whether or not each student had at least one friend who provided a particular resource—emotional support, academic guidance (differentiating planning for the future or assistance with homework), and companionship—in each year of the study.

Peers' encouragement or discouragement of school achievement scales.   In Year 2 of the study (junior high school), Midgley et al.'s (1998) scales of peer encouragement and discouragement of school were added to the Circle of Friends Interview. Respondents rate each item on a 5-point Likert scale, ranging from 1 (*not at all true*) to 5 (*very true*). Examples from the 7-item encouragement scale include: Doing well in school is important to us, and My friends try to get me to do my best in school. Examples from the 6-item discouragement scale include: To be popular with my friends, I sometimes don't try as hard as I could in school, and We're not very interested in school right now. Midgley et al. reported the internal consistency of their scales as $\alpha = .81$; for our sample, reliabilities for the encouragement and discouragement scales were $\alpha = .92$ and $.94$, respectively. For this study, we conceptualized the encouragement scale as an index of peer resources and the discouragement scale as an index of peer challenges.

Academic Achievement

Each year of the larger study, we gathered students' math and English grades and achievement test scores from school records. For this article, the yearly math and English grades served as our measures of academic achievement.

Procedure

Students were interviewed individually in the language of their choice—Spanish or English—during the spring of sixth and seventh grades. The interviews were carried out in quiet spaces at their school, typically an empty classroom or the playground. The interviews, lasting from 30 to 45 min, were audiotaped and transcribed for coding. The interviewer read all questions except for those in the Midgley et al. (1998) scales, which students read independently and completed at their own pace.

Results and Discussion

The results are organized around the four research questions:

1. Are there gender and ethnic differences in friends' emotional support, academic guidance, and companionship during the transition from elementary to junior high school?
2. Is the availability of these three peer resources linked to English and math grades in elementary and junior high school?
3. Are there ethnic and gender differences in junior high school students' perceptions of peers' encouragement or discouragement of school?
4. What is the relation between junior high school students' perceptions of peers' encouragement and discouragement of school and their English and math grades?

In brief, peers' emotional support, academic guidance, and companionship were remarkably similar across ethnic and gender groups. In both elementary (sixth grade, Year 1) and junior high school (seventh grade, Year 2), most students had at least one friend who provided each of these resources. Second, as predicted, the link between these peer resources and grades was stronger in junior high than in elementary school. With regard to junior high school students' perception of peers' overall encouragement and discouragement of school, most students reported moderate support and little discouragement. In contrast to past research, we found little evidence of gender or ethnic differences in these patterns. As predicted, however, junior high school students' perceptions of peers' encouragement and discouragement of school were linked to their English and math grades.

Peers' Provision of Emotional Support, Academic Guidance, and Companionship

The patterns were remarkably similar across gender and ethnicity. Because a central goal of our study was to identify potential explanations of the high rates of academic difficulties and dropout for Latinos relative to European Americans, we aggregated our data across gender to increase the statistical power of our analyses. As evident in Table 1, in most cases at least half the students nominated at least one

TABLE 1
Percent of Students Who Reported That at Least One Friend Provided the Resource as a
Function of Ethnicity and Grade in School

| | Ethnicity | | | |
| | Latino | | European American | |
Resource	6th Grade	7th Grade	6th Grade	7th Grade
Emotional support	63	50	64	52
Guidance with homework	36	27	58	86
Guidance with the future	36	41	53	63
Companionship	95	100	100	100

friend who provided each type of resource. It also appears that in elementary school
(Year 1), students were receiving relatively more emotional support and companionship from friends than either type of academic guidance. Such differences were
not apparent in junior high school (Year 2). Not surprisingly, in both years companionship was the most available resource. Because companionship is a central function of friendship across the life span, access to both emotional support and academic guidance depends on opportunities to spend time with friends.

The 2 (ethnicity: European American or Latino) × 2 (availability of resource:
yes or no) chi-square analyses carried out for each school year yielded only one
significant difference. In junior high school, European American students received more help with their homework than Latino students, $\chi^2(1, N = 102) = 9.63$,
$p < .002$. Although it appears from the table that participants reported more homework and future planning peer resources in Year 2 than in Year 1, the 2 (year: sixth
[elementary] or seventh [junior high]) × 2 (availability of resource: yes or no)
chi-square analyses carried out for emotional resources, academic guidance (future planning and homework assistance), and companionship yielded no significant effects. In sum, concerning our first research question, we found little gender
and ethnic variation in peer resources in either elementary or junior high school.
Moreover, there was little change in the availability of these resources from elementary to junior high school.

Students' academic achievement.   Students' grade point averages
(GPAs) in math and English are presented in Table 2 as a function of their gender,
ethnicity, and year in school. The 2 (gender) × 2 (ethnicity) × 2 (grade: 6 or 7) analyses of variance (ANOVAs) carried out on math and English GPAs showed that European American students had significantly higher math and English GPAs than

TABLE 2
Means and Standard Deviations for Math and English Grades as a Function of Ethnicity, Gender, and Year in School

| | European American | | | | Latino | | | |
| | Girls | | Boys | | Girls | | Boys | |
Measure	M	SD	M	SD	M	SD	M	SD
6th grade								
English GPA	3.52	.60	3.44	.53	2.76	.86	2.38	.83
Math GPA	3.28	.81	3.27	.83	2.45	.81	2.29	.65
7th grade								
English GPA	3.24	.93	2.90	1.10	2.35	.97	1.91	.98
Math GPA	3.17	.96	2.88	.96	2.43	.79	2.58	.93

Note.   GPA = grade point average.

did Latino students in both sixth and seventh grades, $F(1, 75) = 13.14, p < .001$ and $F(1, 94) = 29.67, p < .001$, respectively. Students' math and English GPAs were also highly interrelated, with all correlations above $r = .47, p < .001$. Because tracking minority students in high school away from college-preparatory tracks is a major concern, we assessed potential tracking among our participants. To do so, we examined the English and math classes Latino and European American students took in seventh grade. Because most students from both ethnic groups were enrolled in seventh-grade English, no tracking was evident in this subject. However, tracking in math was indicated by finding that 26% of European American students but no Latino students took prealgebra in seventh grade. Except for 2 students, Latinos were enrolled in seventh-grade math, as were all but 3 of the remaining European American students. These data indicate that Latinos were not being tracked to remedial courses, but that by seventh grade, more European American than Latino students were enrolled in accelerated college-preparatory math.

Links Between Peer Resources and Academic Achievement

Our second question concerned the relation between peer resources and school grades. To test the hypothesis that peer resources would be associated with higher English and math grades, we carried out 2 (availability of resource: yes or no) × 2 (gender) × 2 (ethnicity) × 2 (year of study) ANOVAs on each resource: emotional support, guidance in planning the future, and guidance with homework. Because almost all students reported having at least one friend who provided companionship, we did not analyze these data further. ANOVAs on the other functions revealed no significant gender or ethnic variation. However, ANOVAs on English GPAs did yield the predicted interaction between peer resource and year for emotional support, $F(1, 91) = 20.31, p < .001$, guidance for the future, $F(1, 91) = 28.24, p < .001$, and guidance with homework, $F(1, 91) = 49.49, p < .0001$, respectively. As shown in Table 3, in all cases the availability of peer resources was more strongly related to English GPA in junior high (Year 2) than in elementary school (Year 1). These results highlight the increasing importance of peer resources for school during the transition to adolescence and are consistent with other findings of the importance of friends in adolescents' lives at school (Berndt, 1999; Cooper & Cooper, 1992).

Peers' Encouragement and Discouragement of School

Our third question concerned gender and ethnic variation in junior high students' perceptions of peers' overall encouragement and discouragement of school. Table 4 displays the mean encouragement and discouragement from peers (i.e., peers as resources and as challenges) for school achievement as a function of ethnicity and gender. Students reported moderate levels of encouragement or discouragement from peers. A 2 (gender) × 2 (ethnicity) ANOVA carried out on the encouragement scale indicated that contrary to predictions, European American students did not report more encouragement than Latino students ($F < 1$). The only significant effect was that girls reported more encouragement from their friends than did boys ($Ms = 3.90$ vs. 3.48), $F(1, 97) = 6.64, p < .01$. There were no significant gender or ethnic differences in students' perceptions of their peers' discouragement of schooling. Thus we did not find the hypothesized Gender × Ethnicity interaction. Taken together, the findings suggest that although boys perceived their friends as offering

TABLE 3
Mean English GPA as a Function of the Availability of the Peer Resource and Year of the Study

| | Peer Resource Available | | Peer Resource Not Available | |
Resource	6th Grade	7th Grade	6th Grade	7th Grade
Emotional support	3.24	2.82	3.14	2.66
Guidance with homework	3.18	2.94	3.17	2.13
Guidance with future	3.09	2.84	3.21	2.61

Note.   Analyses were not carried out for companionship because almost all the students had at least one friend who provided companionship. GPA = grade point average.

TABLE 4
Means and (Standard Deviations) of Positive and Negative Peer Support for School as a
Function of Ethnicity and Gender

| | European American | | | | Latino | | | |
| | Girls | | Boys | | Girls | | Boys | |
Measure	M	SD	M	SD	M	SD	M	SD
Positive support	3.90	.73	3.59	.67	3.90	1.03	3.36	2.20
Negative support	1.65	.51	1.84	.49	1.74	.59	1.85	.69

less encouragement of schooling, they did not view friends as actively discouraging academics.

Associations Between Peers' Support and Discouragement for School and English and Math GPA

As predicted, students' perceptions of peers as resources for school were significantly correlated with grades in junior high school math, $r(103) = .27, p < .007$, and English, $r(103) = .31, p < .001$. Also as predicted, perceptions of peers as challenges for school were negatively correlated with grades in junior high school math, $r(103) = -.23, p < .02$, and English, $r(103) = -.33, p < .001$.

Summary

Taken together, the results of Study 1 showed that students perceived their peers primarily as resources and that peer resources were positively related to school grades, whereas perceptions of peers as challenges were negatively related to grades. Although finding little peer discouragement in this early adolescent school-based sample contradicts other work with high school students (Eckert, 1989; Fordham & Ogbu, 1986; Gibson, 1993; Romo & Falbo, 1996; Willis, 1977), minority and low-income students' disenchantment with school and majority culture institutions may not yet have occurred in early junior high school. Study 2, which included older students, allowed us to test this possibility. It is also possible that at least some students already perceived school negatively and were members of more alienated peer groups. In the junior high schools we sampled, Latinos were a minority and some might have felt alienated at a time of life when belonging and fitting in is so important (Seidman, Allen, Aber, Mitchell, & Feinman, 1994). How would peer relationships look in a context where Latino students were the majority and school achievement and college and career planning were encouraged? This was the central question we pursued in Study 2.

STUDY 2

Study 2 examined the role of peers as challenges and resources among middle and high school youth who were participating in a community college outreach program. We asked three questions:

1. Did the youth see peers as resources for and challenges to pursuing their career goals?
2. What were the math pathways from sixth to ninth grades of youth participating in the program?
3. Were peer challenges and resources related to students' elementary school math grades and their pathways to either Algebra 1 or remedial math at ninth grade?

Although peers can foster oppositional identities and alienation, they can also be assets for developing academic and college identities (Mehan et al., 1996). For many youth, friends are the most important reason for attending and staying in school (Cauce et al., 1996). For some, peer pressures to become involved with drugs, sex, and aggression are foreshadowed by older siblings and friends engaging in these behaviors, becoming parents in high school, dropping out of school, and entering the juvenile justice system. Yet under some conditions, these pressures create conflicts that foster exploration of alternative goals and strategies for attaining them. Youniss and Smollar (1985) found that such conflicts and their resolution could stimulate youth, parents, and teachers to renegotiate mutual expectations during the transition through adolescence. This is consistent with our findings with the Bridging Multiple Worlds model that link challenges in the context of support to youths' career and college identity formation (Cooper et al., in press; Cooper, Jackson, Azmitia, Lopez, & Dunbar, 1995).

Still, youth whose families are new to U.S. schools may be particularly vulnerable to challenges from peers who are alienated from school. Studies of Mexican immigrant families, for example, consistently show that youth and their families hold high hopes for moving up from their parents' lives of physical labor to professional careers (Azmitia, Cooper, Garcia, & Dunbar, 1996; Henderson, 1997; Matute-Bianchi, 1991). In essence, they seek to beat the odds and disprove theories of social reproduction—that each society's social class hierarchy tends to be reproduced from generation to generation (Bourdieu & Passeron, 1977). However, immigrant parents worry about their children's peers. Azmitia and Brown (2000) found that parents of Mexican descent viewed peers as the greatest challenge to their children's future, although parents who believed that their children's friends shared the family's values about education and morality felt more confident about their children's potential for success. For these reasons, researchers have begun to study how community programs can foster positive peer relationships as assets for youth development (Adger, 2001/this issue; Collignon, Men, & Tan, 2001/this issue; Cooper et al., 1995; Eccles, 1999).

Math Pathways to College

Enrollment in math courses provides a key index of students' prospects for future college eligibility and career opportunities, in part because they are easy for stakeholders, including employers, to benchmark, as seen in the nationwide focus on students completing algebra by eighth or ninth grade. Ethnic group differences in high school math pathways are well documented, with Asian American students tending to take more advanced college-preparatory math classes than European American students, and both groups taking more college-preparatory math than African American or Latino students (Catsambis, 1994). Recent research moves beyond describing ethnic group differences to trace variation and change over time within ethnic groups and similarities across them. These studies also map conditions under which ethnic minority students find pathways to college and college-based careers (Cooper et al., in press).

California provides a key context for investigating how ethnically diverse youth navigate their worlds of peers, family, school, and community on their pathways to college. California's Latino population is growing rapidly, especially among school-age youth, with the majority of Latino adults having less than a high school education. California law mandates that the top 12.5% of high school graduates be considered eligible for the University of California, the top 33% eligible for California state universities, and that all 18-year-olds and all high school graduates be considered eligible for California community colleges.

The middle and high school students in Study 2 were youth from mostly Latino, low-income families. They were participating in a community college outreach program that awards $1,000 scholarships to community college. The program offers tutoring by college students, Saturday and summer academies, parent involvement activities, and academic guidance from sixth grade through high school to help at-risk students stay on track to college. Because Algebra 1 is the only math required for the Associate's degree in Arts from California community colleges, the outreach program could be considered selective but not as competitive as university outreach programs that target students likely to be eligible for university admission as indicated by their having taken Algebra 1 by ninth grade as well as completing geometry and Algebra 2 in high school. Our study contributes to an emerging literature that links research, policy, and practice by tracing how ethnically diverse youth navigate their math pathways to community college and 4-year institutions (Cooper et al., in press).

In sum, Study 2 asked three questions. First, we asked whether youth in a community college outreach program saw peers as among their challenges and resources in reaching their career and college goals. We compared students who named peers and families and explored differences among middle school and high school youth. Second, we traced the pathways of program youth in their math classes and grades from sixth to ninth grades. Both university researchers and the program director wanted to monitor students' grades and their eligibility for the university and community college. Third, we asked how peer challenges and resources were related to students' math pathways. Comparing students making higher grades with those doing less well, we predicted that students making both higher and lower grades would see peers as challenges, but that those passing Algebra 1 by ninth grade would be more likely to view peers as resources.

Method

Participants

The sample included 116 students (76 girls and 40 boys) who entered the program between sixth and seventh grade (M age = 11.5 years) from 1995 to 1997. The majority of students were Latino, and almost all were of Mexican descent, with smaller numbers from Central America; 38% were born in Mexico and 62% in the United States; almost all had immigrant parents. All students in the program were required to be from low-income families, as indicated by their eligibility for federal free and reduced-price lunch programs at their schools. Students and their families who participated in the study signed consent forms—written in Spanish and English—as part of a university–community research partnership with the program.

Students' parents worked primarily in manual labor—picking strawberries, lettuce, or mushrooms; working in canneries or factory assembly lines; or cleaning homes, offices, and hotels. The Latino students in the Study 2 community program sample resembled the Latino students in the Study 1 school-based sample in their families' histories of immigration from Mexico, parents' occupation in semi-skilled and unskilled jobs, and students' math grades at sixth grade, which averaged slightly under 3.0 or a B grade (Brown, Cooper, & Azmitia, in press).

The program.   The community college outreach program began in 1991 to increase low-income students' access to college. The founder, inspired by Lang's "I Have a Dream" Program (Kahne, 1999), built an endowment from private donors, both individuals and businesses, and developed partnerships with families and five local middle and junior high schools, to which donors designated scholarships. Once a year, the program director and teachers at each school chose recipients and alternates on the basis of sixth-grade students' application essays and their academic potential, motivation, and grades. In their essays, youth described their career goals, challenges and obstacles to achieving them, and how they would contribute to their communities in the future. Students wrote in Spanish or English about their goals of becoming doctors, lawyers, nurses, and teachers, as well as secretaries, police officers, fire fighters, and mechanics (Cooper et al., 1999).

Measures

As part of our partnership with the program, we adapted the Multiple Worlds Measure (Cooper, Jackson, Azmitia, Lopez, & Dunbar, 1994) into activities for the annual Summer Institute. All materials were written in English and Spanish. The activities included charting career pyramids or time lines of students' career and personal goals and their challenges and resources, mapping networks of who helps and who causes them difficulties across key issues, and graphing their math pathways of classes and grades toward Algebra 1 and college eligibility.

Challenges and resources to career goals.   As part of a leadership class in the program's Summer Institute, students completed the career pyramid activity ($N = 77$ in 1997 and $N = 84$ in 1998). Students wrote their career goal at the top of the pyramid, the steps they planned for each year to attain their goal, and the challenges and resources they experienced and anticipated for each step. The responses, all open-ended, were transcribed and coded inductively.

School classes and grades.   Students' classes and their grades were obtained from transcripts from each student's school. These were collected by program staff as part of their partnerships with participating schools. Two variables were coded: students' math grades at the time they entered the program and, for 30 students, whether or not they passed Algebra 1 by ninth grade.

Results and Discussion

We summarize our findings with regard to the three questions of Study 2:

1. Did middle and high school youth in the community college outreach program see peers as among their challenges and resources in reaching their career goals?

2. What were the math pathways of the program youth from sixth to ninth grades?
3. How were peer challenges and resources related to students' pathways?

In brief, youth saw peers as both challenges and resources in reaching their career goals, and as greater challenges than their families. High school youth in one Summer Institute cohort saw peers as greater challenges than did younger youth. Second, at ninth grade, students' math pathways (which had not reflected tracking at sixth grade) split between Algebra 1 and remedial classes; these pathways could be predicted by students' grades in sixth-grade math. Third, students' reports of peer challenges and resources were modestly related to their math pathways, with those making higher math grades in sixth grade more likely to name peers as resources for one cohort. Our finding that students in both algebra and remedial classes experienced peers as challenges and resources holds implications for building inclusive opportunities for college and college-based careers.

Peers: Challenges or Resources?

Among the challenges and resources students listed on their career pyramids were their families, peers, school, themselves, money, and the program. In both 1997 (N = 77) and 1998 (N = 84), students listed peers as challenges and resources at comparable rates (30% vs. 40% of students in 1997 and 50% vs. 55% in 1998). More specifically, students described their challenges by listing boyfriends, girlfriends, peer pressure, gangs, temptation of friends dropping out, friends as bad examples, bad friends, bigger students, illegal friends, and enemies. Many also listed drugs, sex, having babies, or pregnancies. In 1997, youth in high school listed peers as challenges more than youth in middle or junior high school, $\chi^2(1, N = 66) = 7.25, p < .007$. As resources, students also listed friends, boyfriends, girlfriends, bigger students, and "leaving your boyfriend if he takes too much time." In contrast, students were much more likely to list their families as resources than as challenges (70% vs. 10%, respectively, in 1997, and 73% vs. 10% in 1998).

Pathways to Algebra and College

To trace the relation of students' challenges and resources to their math pathways through school, we followed 30 Summer Institute participants from the year they entered the program at sixth or seventh grade through ninth grade. More than half (N = 18) had taken and passed Algebra 1 with a grade of C or better, a key step on their pathway to eligibility for 4-year colleges and universities. None had taken Algebra 1 in eighth grade (the accelerated pattern shown by a sizable number of European American students in Study 1). Of the remaining 12 students, 5 failed algebra at ninth grade and 7 took remedial math classes that year. Each of these students was eligible for community college, where Algebra 1 is the only math required for an Associate's degree in Arts. These pathways diverged early: Students who passed Algebra 1 at ninth grade had made higher math grades in sixth grade than students who failed algebra or took remedial classes (Ms = 3.26 and 2.43, respectively), $t(28) = 2.6, p < .02$.

What Roles Do Peers Have in Math Pathways?

We tested our hypothesis that students doing better in school would view peers as challenges and resources differently than would students making lower grades in two stages. First, we compared reports of peers as challenges and resources from 114 students who attended the Summer Institute in relation to their sixth-grade math grades. Students who listed peers as challenges did not differ on sixth-grade math grades from those who did not (Ms = 2.87 vs. 2.86, ns). In other words, stronger and weaker students were equally likely to name peers as challenges. With regard to resources, for students attending the Summer Institute in 1998 (but not 1997), those making higher grades at sixth grade were more likely to name peers as resources compared to those not naming peers as resources (Ms = 3.52 and 2.33, respectively), $t(25) = 3.16, p < .004$. Students who passed algebra at ninth grade were as likely to list peers as both resources and challenges as students in remedial classes. Therefore, the hypothesis that students doing better in school would have access to more resources from peers was supported only modestly.

Thus, like our research with African American and Latino youth in competitive university outreach programs, students in this selective community college outreach program reported challenges as well as resources across the contexts of their lives, with peer relationships being the most controversial (Cooper et al., in press). The role of peers as assets, including ties formed across ethnic, gender, and social class lines, deserves further attention for youth struggling to create viable peer and academic identities (Hamm, 1998). In our current work, we are examining whether ties with peers within and across ethnic, gender, and social class groups translate into benefits in schooling, although youth in Study 2 attended predominantly Latino schools, thereby restricting opportunities for such ties. In research with adults, Gándara and Osugi (1994) found that successful Chicana professionals recalled how friendships with Anglo students helped them learn about college, and Henze (2001/this issue) reports growing interest in enhancing conditions in schools for cross-ethnic ties among students, families, and school staff.

CONCLUSIONS AND FUTURE DIRECTIONS

This research investigated the role of peers and community programs in European American and Latino adolescent students' academic achievement and educational and career goals. The open-ended, emic approach used in Study 2 showed that peers figure prominently in youths' ideas of the resources and challenges that promote or hinder school achievement and help them stay on track to college. Study 1 allowed us to test specific predictions about the types of resources students draw from peers and the ways peers encourage or discourage achievement. Because the students in Study 2 were more specific about the ways peers challenged their schooling, we do not know if they conceptualized peer resources in terms of the concepts of emotional support, academic guidance, and companionship we used in Study 1. Interestingly, the peer challenges that students in Study 2 listed were remarkably similar to those expressed by parents of the students in Study 1: sex, drugs, violence, and academic discouragement (see Azmitia & Brown, 2000). These may represent widespread risks of adolescent peer relationships and indicate that parents' concerns are based on their own experiences and those of their children. The students' reports suggest that to an extent, parents' fears were justified.

Study 1, but not Study 2, showed that students' perceptions of their peers' emotional support, academic guidance, and companionship and their perceptions of peers' overall encouragement and discouragement of school were associated with their grades, with more students reporting encouragement to do better in school than those reporting discouragement. Thus, our research establishes a link between peer resources and challenges and school achievement. Because the result was not consistent across the two studies, however, more research examining this link is essential.

Study 2 revealed that peers, more than families, were sources of both challenges and resources to youth in the program. This finding suggests that help from others in taking advantage of resources while resisting challenges would be valuable. Community organizations such as the outreach program we studied can help ethnic minority students succeed in school, not only by providing academic support and guidance for the future but also opportunities to spend time with friends in a supportive environment. Thus, programs might offset some of the academic and social costs of tracking that begins in junior high school. Of course, to benefit from programs, students must stay engaged in them. Unfortunately, attrition in attendance was high. As students moved through adolescence, sports, romantic partners, and work drew them away from program activities, although small numbers of high school youth attended as chaperons for younger siblings or in leadership roles as tutors.

Although students in Study 1 did not see peers as particularly challenging to their school achievement and future goals, those in Study 2 did report negative pressures from peers, and the perceptions of peer challenges were greater among high school youth. In junior high school, peer discouragement for school may not be as active as in high school, the focus of most reports of negative effects of peers on minority students' academic success (Eckert, 1989; Fordham & Ogbu, 1986; Gibson, 1993; Willis, 1977). However, this possibility should not obscure the fact that youth in both studies reported encouragement of school from peers, and that, in Study 1, this support was correlated with school grades in junior high school. In our future research, we will use comparative case study methods to investigate the academic pathways of Latino and European American boys and girls receiving high levels of encouragement or discouragement of academic achievement and identity from their friends.

In Study 2, peer challenges and resources were examined among students on two pathways through school: those making steadily high grades in classes leading to university eligibility and those taking remedial math classes leading to community college. A key finding was that students' math pathways had diverged into college and remedial classes, in contrast to students in more competitive programs such as AVID that focus on students scoring above the median (Gándara et al., 1998). For students in remedial classes, attending the college outreach program and being treated as "at promise" for college rather than as at risk for dropping out of school might enhance their engagement and persistence in school. Finding these two college pathways is particularly noteworthy given research that African American and Latino students in remedial and vocational classes are more pessimistic, disengaged, and alienated as they move through school, whereas youth in gifted and college-preparatory classes not surprisingly report more support and optimism about the future (Ford & Harris, 1996; Gibson, 1997). Our findings indicate that in addition to more competitive university outreach programs like AVID and EAOP, more inclusive programs for community colleges are assets in communities. For all of these programs, both families and peers are key resources with which effective programs would do well to engage on behalf of students' school success (Azmitia, Brown, & Cooper, in press).

Finally, these two studies of how low-income youth develop in the context of peer relationships in schools and community programs hold implications for sociocultural theory and the bridging multiple worlds model, which both consider personal, interpersonal, institutional, and community levels of development over time. For example, we observed that just as the youth were struggling to negotiate and navigate their own relationships and pathways through school, the outreach program—like other community programs and partnerships across the nation—continued to struggle for funding and space (see Adger, 2001/this issue). As a private–public partnership, its challenges in turn constrained the resources available to youth and their families. Such findings point to the importance of mapping challenges and resources across individuals, relationships, institutions, and communities to sustain engagement on behalf of diverse youth and their opportunities in school.

ACKNOWLEDGMENTS

This work was supported by grants to the authors from the U.S. Department of Education Office of Educational Research and Improvement (PR/Award

R306A60001), through the Center for Research on Education, Diversity and Excellence, Santa Cruz, California, as administered by the Office of Educational Research and Improvement (OERI), National Institute on the Education of At-Risk Students (NIEARS), and the U.S. Department of Education (USDOE), and to Catherine R. Cooper from the John D. and Catherine T. MacArthur Foundation Research Network on Successful Pathways through Middle Childhood.

We wish to thank the youth, families, schools, and outreach program for participating, and Gregory Thrush, Maria Carillo, Lissa Pearlman, and Mary Jo Rollins for assisting with data for Study 1. We also thank Elizabeth Domínguez, Jill Denner, Edward M. Lopez, Nora Dunbar, Gabriela Chavira, and Wendy Rivera for their many contributions to Study 2.

The contents, finding, and opinions expressed in this article are those of the authors and do not necessarily represent the positions or policies of its funding sources.

REFERENCES

Adger, C. T. (2001/this issue). School–community-based organization partnerships for language minority students' school success. *Journal of Education for Students Placed At Risk, 6.*

Azmitia, M., & Brown, J. R. (2000, April). *Latino immigrant parents' beliefs about the "path of life" for their adolescent children.* Paper presented at the Kent State University Forum, Latino Children and Families in the United States, Kent, OH.

Azmitia, M., Brown, J. R., & Cooper, C. R. (in press). *Familism in action: The relation between family guidance and emotional support and adolescents' academic achievement during the transition from elementary to junior high school.*

Azmitia, M., & Cooper, C. R. (1996). *Navigating and negotiating home, school, peer, and community linkages in adolescence.* Santa Cruz, CA: U.S. Center for Research On Education, Diversity and Excellence.

Azmitia, M., Cooper, C. R., Garcia, E. E., & Dunbar. N. (1996). The ecology of family guidance in low-income Mexican-American and European-American families. *Social Development, 5,* 1–23.

Azmitia, M., Cooper, C. R., Wishard, A., Thrush, G., & Ittel, A. (1998). *Circle of friends interview.* Santa Cruz: University of California, Santa Cruz.

Azmitia, M., Ittel, A., & Kamprath, N. (1997). *Early adolescence friendship interview.* Santa Cruz: University of California, Santa Cruz.

Berndt, T. J. (1999). Friends' influence on children's adjustment to school. In W. Collins & B. Laursen (Eds.), *Relationships as developmental contexts: The Minnesota Symposium on child psychology* (Vol. 30, pp. 85–107). Mahwah, NJ: Lawrence Erlbaum Associates, Inc.

Berndt, T. J., & Keefe, K. (1995). Friends' influence on adolescents' adjustment to school. *Child Development, 66,* 1312–1329.

Berndt, T. J., Laychak, A. E., & Park, K. (1990). Friends' influence on adolescents' academic achievement and motivation: An experimental study. *Journal of Educational Psychology, 82,* 664–670.

Bourdieu, P., & Passeron, C. (1977). *Reproduction in education, society and culture.* London: Sage.

Brown, B. B. (1990). Peer groups and peer cultures. In S. S. Feldman & G. R. Elliott (Eds.), *At the threshold: The developing adolescent* (pp. 171–196). Cambridge, MA: Harvard University Press.

Brown, J., Cooper, C. R., & Azmitia, M. (in press). *Educación and the path of life among Mexican immigrant families.* Paper presented at the MacArthur Conference on Discovering Successful Pathways in Children's Development: Mixed Methods in the Study of Childhood and Family Life, Santa Monica, CA.

Bukowski, W. M., Newcomb, A. F., & Hartup, W. W. (1996). *The company they keep: Friendship in childhood and adolescence.* New York: Cambridge University Press.

Catsambis, S. (1994). The path to math: Gender and racial-ethnic differences in mathematics participation from middle school to high school. *Sociology of Education, 67,* 199–215.

Cauce, A. M., Mason, C., Gonzales, N., Hiraga, U., & Liu, G. (1996). Social support during adolescence: Methodological and theoretical considerations. In K. Hurrelman & S. F. Hamilton (Eds.), *Social problems and social contexts in adolescents: Perspectives across boundaries* (pp. 131–152). New York: Aldine de Gruyter.

Collignon, F. F., Men, M., & Tan, S. (2001/this issue). Finding ways in: Community-based perspectives on southeast Asian family involvement with schools in a New England state. *Journal of Education for Students Placed At Risk, 6.*

Cooper, C. R., & Cooper, R. G. (1992). Links between adolescents' relationships with their parents and peers: Models, evidence, and mechanisms. In R. D. Parke & G. W. Ladd (Eds.), *Family–peer relationships: Modes of linkages* (pp. 135–158). Hillsdale, NJ: Lawrence Erlbaum Associates, Inc.

Cooper, C. R., Cooper, R. G., Azmitia, M., Chavira, G., & Gullatt, Y. (in press). Bridging multiple worlds: How African American and Latino youth in academic outreach programs navigate math pathways to college. *Applied Developmental Science.*

Cooper, C. R., Denner, J., & Lopez, E. M. (1999). Cultural brokers: Helping Latino children on pathways towards success. *The Future of Children, 9,* 51–57.

Cooper, C. R., Jackson, J. F., Azmitia, M., & Lopez, E. M. (1998). Multiple selves, multiple worlds: Ethnically sensitive research on identity, relationships, and opportunity structures in adolescence. In V. McLoyd & L. Steinberg (Eds.), *Conceptual and methodological issues in the study of minority adolescents and their families* (pp. 111–126). Hillsdale, NJ: Lawrence Erlbaum Associates, Inc.

Cooper, C. R., Jackson, J. F., Azmitia, M., Lopez, E. M., & Dunbar, N. (1994). *Multiple selves, multiple worlds survey: Qualitative and quantitative versions.* Santa Cruz: University of California, Santa Cruz.

Cooper, C. R., Jackson, J. F., Azmitia, M., Lopez, E. M., & Dunbar, N. (1995). Bridging students' multiple worlds: African American and Latino youth in academic outreach programs. In R. F. Macías & R. G. Ramos (Eds.), *Changing schools for changing students: An anthology of research on language minorities* (pp. 243–267). Santa Barbara: University of California Linguistic Minority Research Institute.

Delgado-Gaitán, C. (1986). Adolescent peer influence and differential school performance. *Journal of Adolescent Research, 1,* 103–114.

Eccles, J. S. (1999). The development of children ages 6 to 14. *The Future of Children, 9,* 30–44.

Eckert, P. (1989). *Jocks and burnouts: Social categories and identity in the high school.* New York: Teachers College Press.

Ford, D. Y., & Harris, J. J. (1996). Perceptions and attitudes of Black students toward school, achievement, and other educational variables. *Child Development, 67,* 1141–1152.

Fordham, S., & Ogbu, J. U. (1986). Black students' school success: Coping with the "burden of 'acting White.'" *The Urban Review, 18,* 176–206.

Gándara, P. (1995). *Over the ivy walls: The educational mobility of low-income Chicanos.* Albany: State University of New York Press.

Gándara, P., Larson, K., Mehan, H., & Rumberger, R. (1998). *Capturing Latino students in the academic pipeline* (Rep. No. 1). Sacramento, CA: Chicano/Latino Policy Project.

Gándara, P., & Osugi, L. (1994). Educationally ambitious Chicanas. *The NEA Higher Education Journal, 10,* 7–35.

Gibson, M. A. (1993). The school performance of immigrant minorities: A comparative view. In E. Jacob & C. Jordan (Eds.), *Minority education: Anthropological perspectives* (pp. 113–128). Norwood, NJ: Ablex.

Gibson, M. A. (Ed.). (1997). Ethnicity and school performance: Complicating the immigrant/involuntary minority typology [Special issue]. *Anthropology and Education Quarterly, 28*(3).

Gonzalez, N., Andrade, R., Civil, M., & Moll, L. (2001/this issue). Bridging funds of distributed knowledge: Creating zones of practices in mathematics. *Journal of Education for Students Placed At Risk, 6*(1).

Greenfield, P. M., & Cocking, R. R. (1994). *Cross-cultural roots of minority child development.* Hillsdale, NJ: Lawrence Erlbaum Associates, Inc.

Hamm, J. V. (1998). Negotiating the maze: Adolescents' cross-ethnic peer relations in ethnically diverse schools. In L. H. Meyer, H. S. Park, M. Grenot-Scheyer, I. S. Schwartz, & B. Harry (Eds.), *Making friends: The influences of culture and development* (pp. 243–262). Baltimore: Brookes-Cole.

Henderson, R. W. (1997). Educational and occupational aspirations and expectations among parents of middle school students of Mexican descent: Family resources for academic development and mathematics learning. In R. D. Taylor & M. C. Wang (Eds.), *Social and emotional adjustment and family relationships in ethnic minority families* (pp. 99–131). Mahwah, NJ: Lawrence Erlbaum Associates, Inc.

Henze, R. C. (2001/this issue). Segregated classrooms, integrated intent: How one school struggled to develop positive interethnic relations. *Journal of Education for Students Placed At Risk, 6,* 133–155.

Hollingshead, A. B., & Redlich, F. C. (1958). *Social class and mental illness.* New York: Wiley.

Hymel, S., Comfort, C., Schonert-Reichl, K., & McDougall, P. (1996). Academic failure and school dropout: The influence of peers. In J. Juvonen & K. R. Wentzel (Eds.), *Social motivation: Understanding children's school adjustment* (pp. 313–345). New York: Cambridge University Press.

Jacob, E., & Jordan, C. (1993). *Minority education: Anthropological perspectives.* Norwood, NJ: Ablex.

Kahne, J. (1999). Personalized philanthropy: Can it support youth and build civic commitments? *Youth and Society, 30,* 367–387.

Larson, K., & Rumberger, R. (1995). Doubling school success in highest-risk Latino youth: Results from a middle school intervention study. In R. F. Macías & R. G. Garcia-Ramos (Eds.), *Changing schools for changing families: An anthology of research on language minorities, schools, and society* (pp. 157–180). Santa Barbara: University of California Linguistic Minority Research Institute.

Matute-Bianchi, M. E. (1991). Situational ethnicity and patterns of school performance among immigrant and non-immigrant Mexican descent students. In M. A. Gibson & J. U. Ogbu (Eds.), *Minority status and schooling: A comparative study of immigrant and involuntary minorities* (pp. 205–248). New York: Garland.

Mehan, H., Villanueva, I., Hubbard, L., & Lintz, A. (1996). *Constructing school success: The consequences of untracking low achieving students.* Cambridge, MA: Cambridge University Press.

Midgley, C., Kaplan, A., Middleton, M., Maehr, M. L., Urdan, T., Anderman, L. H., & Roeser, R. (1998). The development and validation of scales assessing students' achievement goal orientations. *Contemporary Educational Psychology, 23,* 113–131.

Moll, L., & Whitmore, K. F. (1993). Vygotsky in classroom practice: Moving from individual transmission to social transaction. In E. A. Forman, N. Minick, & C. Addison Stone (Eds.), *Contexts for learning: Sociocultural dynamics in children's development* (pp. 19–42). New York: Oxford University Press.

Phelan, P., Davidson, A. L., & Yu, H. C. (1991). Students' multiple worlds: Navigating the borders of family, peer, and school cultures. In P. Phelan & A. L. Davidson (Eds.), *Cultural diversity: Implications for education* (pp. 52–88). New York: Teachers College Press.

Rogoff, B. (1998). Cognition as a collaborative process. In D. Kuhn & R. S. Siegler (Vol. Eds.) & W. Damon (Series Ed.), *Handbook of child psychology: Vol. 2. Cognition, perception, and language* (pp. 679–744). New York: Wiley.

Romo, H. D., & Falbo, T. (1996). *Latino high school graduation: Defying the odds.* Austin: University of Texas Press.

Seidman, E., Allen, L. R., Aber, J., Mitchell, C., & Feinman, J. (1994). The impact of school transitions in early adolescence on the self-system and perceived social context of poor urban youth. *Child Development, 65,* 507–522.

Tharp, R. G., & Gallimore, R. (1988). *Rousing minds to life: Teaching learning and schooling in social context.* Cambridge, MA: Cambridge University Press.

Willis, P. (1977). *Learning to labour: How working class kids get working class jobs.* Westmead, England: Saxon House.

Youniss, J., & Smollar, J. (1985). *Adolescent relations with mothers, fathers, and friends.* Chicago: University of Chicago Press.

JOURNAL OF EDUCATION FOR STUDENTS PLACED AT RISK, 6(1&2), 73–93
Copyright © 2001, Lawrence Erlbaum Associates, Inc.

Planning for the Future in Rural and Urban High Schools

Patricia Gándara, Dianna Gutiérrez, and Susan O'Hara
Division of Education
University of California, Davis

Studies of postsecondary aspirations tend to assume that adolescents from different ethnic groups share commonalities of perspective that are unaffected by the areas in which they live and go to school. Largely missing from this literature is a consideration of the intersection of ethnicity, development, and location. This study looks at the ways in which White and Latino students in an urban and a rural high school differ in their perspectives on postsecondary plans according to grade level, ethnicity, and urbanicity. We find a number of differences in student attitudes and behavior depending on whether students attend rural or urban high schools. High school experiences are also moderated by ethnicity across locations. However, with respect to how students want others to see them, students in the rural high school are more like each other than they are like their ethnic counterparts in the urban school. We conclude that, in many respects, both Latino and White students experience schooling and adolescent development differently in rural and urban schools.

Many factors influence a young person's decision about post-high school plans. For most adolescents, parents and family members will have a major impact on this decision (Brown & Theobald, 1998; Cooper & Cooper, 1992; Steinberg, 1996), but we also know that schools, peers, and communities contribute to this important decision and have independent effects (National Research Council, 1993; Steinberg, Brown, Cider, Kaczmarek, & Lazzaro, 1988). However, we know relatively little about how these influences differ across ethnic groups and geographic contexts. Steinberg (1996) and others (Steinberg, Dornbusch, & Brown, 1992) have presented survey data that suggest that Asian peers are more supportive of academic achievement than other groups, and that White and Asian parents also support aca-

---

Requests for reprints should be sent to Patricia Gándara, Division of Education, University of California, One Shields Avenue, Davis, CA 95616–8579. E-mail: pcgandara@ucdavis.edu

demic goals more effectively than parents of Black and Latino youngsters. Others (Fordham & Ogbu, 1986, Matute-Bianchi, 1986) have noted that the peers of some Black and Latino adolescents may send disapproving messages to students who excel in school. Thus, these students may downplay their academic abilities in an attempt to fit in, resulting in altered postsecondary aspirations. Other researchers (Brown & Theobald, 1998; Cooper & Cooper, 1992; Gándara, 1995) have shown that peers can exert a positive or supportive influence on academic achievement. Kao and Tienda (1998) found that although postsecondary aspirations may be uniformly high for all groups of high school students, Asian and White students appear to be consistently more successful in realizing them, as their aspirations tend to be more closely tied to their actual academic achievement.

Most large-scale studies of adolescent achievement behavior and postsecondary aspirations treat their data as if high-school-age students are relatively similar in their perspectives and often combine responses from students across grade levels. Studies of postsecondary aspirations also tend to assume that adolescents from different ethnic groups share commonalities of perspective that are unaffected by the areas in which they live and go to school. Largely missing from this literature is a consideration of the intersection of ethnicity, development, and location. Thus many questions remain unanswered about the development of achievement aspirations among ethnically diverse youth. One of these questions is the impact of development on the process of making postsecondary decisions. Another is the role of residential location in forming attitudes toward post-high-school plans. For example, Latino high school students in urban settings are often presumed to share similar perspectives with Latino students from rural settings. In the study presented here, we challenge this assumption.

THEORETICAL PERSPECTIVES ON ADOLESCENT DEVELOPMENT AND ASPIRATIONS

Adolescence is intimately associated with the process of identity development (Erikson, 1968; Marcia, 1980; Swanson, Spencer, & Petersen, 1998), and many researchers have suggested that this is a period of particular stress and turmoil, especially for young adolescents who are also undergoing major physical changes (Csikszentmihalyi & Schmidt, 1998; Eccles et al., 1993). Erikson (1968) described the primary task of adolescence as one of trying on different personas in a search for an integrated ego identity. As adolescents experiment with different "possible selves" (Markus & Nurius, 1986), they draw from their own sociohistorical contexts and the significant others in their environment for prototypes of role possibilities. Usually this involves parents and other family members, peers, and, to a lesser extent, school personnel and other members of their community (Brown & Theobald, 1998; Cooper, Jackson, Azmitia, Lopez, & Dunbar, 1995; Phelan, Davidson, & Cao, 1991). For young people in the mainstream of society, the opinions and perceptions of these different individuals will vary in predictable ways and be mediated in the normal course of development (Cooper & Cooper, 1992; Grotevant & Cooper, 1985). However, for some ethnic minority youth, there may be such variance in the expectations among these individuals that it is difficult to navigate these multiple worlds in a successful search for a stable identity (Phelan et al., 1991). For these adolescents, peer acceptance may require a persona so distinctly different from that expected by parents from traditional cultures that both internal and external conflicts can result, with high costs for social and personal outcomes (Stanton-Salazar, in press).

Csikszentmihalyi and Schmidt (1998) suggested that genetic encoding necessarily results in conflicts with the social environment for many adolescents. Although adolescents are genetically programmed to engage in socially aggressive behaviors and sexual experimentation, healthy adaptation to adult society necessarily involves restricting these behaviors. With few socially sanctioned alternative outlets for these biologically normal behaviors, Csikszentmihalyi and Schmidt suggested that it is not surprising that adolescents are prone to run afoul of adult rules and expectations. However, most adolescents survive the "storm" of this developmental period and emerge with a reasonably stable sense of self that propels them on to the next stage of human development, the search for intimacy. Those who do not weather these storms successfully, however, are disproportionately from lower income and marginalized groups where healthy alternative avenues for adolescent expression are less common in neighborhoods and communities (National Research Council, 1993). For example, Foley (1990) demonstrated how the same rebellious adolescent behavior was perceived as normal by the White community when it occurred among White adolescents, but was viewed as an expression of deviance when it occurred among Mexican American and other marginalized youth in a south Texas community.

The identity that adolescents negotiate during their high school years not only has major implications for their personal and social adaptation to adult society, but will also lay the foundation for future educational and occupational choices that will circumscribe their life course. Adolescents who are encouraged to see themselves as smart and academically competent are far more likely to have high postsecondary school aspirations than are those who either do not see their identity as closely connected to school (e.g., students who reject the culture of schooling through truancy or dropping out) or are perceived as unsuccessful in school (Kao & Tienda, 1998). Unfortunately, adolescents' ethnic group membership plays a significant role in whether they are seen as academically competent and therefore might come to see themselves in this light. Black and Latino adolescents are more likely to be stereotyped as underachievers than White and Asian youngsters (Kao & Tienda, 1998). Thus, the process of identity formation and the resulting life changes take on different characteristics depending on the ethnic background of the student.

Gender also plays a role in identity development, and considerable research has been devoted to the ways in which girls have been socialized to see themselves as less academically competent than boys (Sadker & Sadker, 1994). Although substantial change has occurred in recent years, often girls are still stereotyped as best at nurturing roles and occupations, and boys as excelling in roles that require more aggressive and autonomous behaviors (Kimmel & Rudolph, 1998). Thus, the process of identity development differs in significant ways for boys and girls.

Recent studies that have explored issues of adolescent choices and well-being have found that family connectedness as well as a sense of belonging at school are protective factors that mitigate against adolescents engaging in risky behaviors (Carnegie Council on Adolescent Development, 1995; Resnick et al., 1997). Nonetheless, low-income students, ethnic minorities, and young people growing up in high-risk neighborhoods are especially in danger of having difficult transitions into adulthood, even when parent involvement and concern are high (National Research Council, 1993).

PERSPECTIVES ON THE ROLE OF GEOGRAPHICAL LOCATION IN THE FORMATION OF ASPIRATIONS

Most poor and minority students are clustered in the inner cities (National Center for Education Statistics, 1999). In California, where this study took place, urban schools have twice the proportion of poor students as suburban schools, and rural schools fall somewhere in between (Betts, Rueben, & Danenberg, 2000). For this reason, most of the focus in the literature on schooling and minorities has centered on urban schools, and a substantial amount is known about these schools and the students in them. Relatively little is known, however, about rural communities and schools and the ways in which they contribute to the aspirations of their youth. Research in rural settings has proven to be a challenge (Carmichael, 1982; DeYoung, 1992; Khattri, Riley, & Kane, 1997; Stern, 1994). Some of the difficulty arises because there is no agreement on what constitutes rural. There is great diversity among the states in the characteristics of their rural populations. Thus, a majority of what we do know about rural schools comes from national data (Stern, 1994). In 1993–1994, of approximately 83,621 public elementary and secondary schools in the United States, 26% were located in rural areas and enrolled 16% of the student population. Unfortunately, most research on rural schools is demographically descriptive but sheds little light on the ways in which these schools may differ in their operations and modes of influence from those in either urban or suburban areas. Thus, the theoretical literature is relatively undeveloped and our understandings of the effects of geography on student aspirations are generally atheoretical and based on scant data. The stereotype of the rural school is that it exists in a bucolic setting, both buffered from the concerns of urban America and isolated from the social advantages of suburbia. Thus, although rural students may live according to a differ-ent rhythm, they are nonetheless perceived to be protected from the more virulent behaviors of inner-city youth. Data show, however, that certain risk behaviors, such as emotional distress and sexual activity, may actually be higher among rural adolescents than among their urban and suburban peers (Resnick et al., 1997). Ru-ral schools may also suffer from real limitations based on the fact that economies of scale cannot be realized, so that many things are more costly, and lower tax bases yield less income. Lack of sufficient resources can translate into limited curricular and programmatic offerings, lower teacher salaries, and insufficient technological resources. As a consequence, rural students may not receive the quality curriculum and education they need to compete nationally and globally (Khattri et al., 1997). Data on course offerings in the 1980s suggest that half of urban schools and two thirds of suburban schools offered calculus, as compared with one third of rural schools. Such data also indicate that the number of courses and special programs offered to rural students is much smaller than those offered to suburban students (Ballou & Podgursky, 1995). A recent California study of school resources and stu-dent outcomes, however, found that on every indicator of schooling outcomes, ru-ral students compared favorably to urban students, but fell far below suburbanites (Betts et al., 2000).

On the other hand, recent studies of school size suggest that the typical size of a rural school is far more ideal for fostering healthy social and emotional growth than the typical suburban or urban school of more than 2,000 students (National Center for Education Statistics, 1999). This research also suggests that the benefits of smaller schools may outweigh the liabilities associated with reduced curricular offerings. Researchers have found that students in small schools fared better than their peers in large schools on a host of outcome indicators. Students from smaller schools had greater voluntary participation in extracurricular activities, a greater sense of obligation, more feelings of satisfaction and sense of belonging, less lone-liness, and less use of drugs and alcohol (Fowler & Walberg, as cited in Stern, 1994).

Dropout rates for rural students tend to be lower than those for urban students. Between 1987 and 1989, the dropout rate for rural students was 13.4%, whereas in urban settings it was 15.3% (Khattri et al., 1997). Although rural schools have lower dropout rates, due to the high incidence of rural poverty, fewer students who do drop out ever return to complete their education (Sherman, 1992; Stern, 1994). In addition, fewer high school graduates aspire to go on to college. Among seniors in 1992, 71% of rural students reported plans to go to college right after high school, compared to 78% of urban and suburban students (Khattri et al., 1997). The extent to which these discrepancies are due to socioeconomic factors or loca-tion factors is highly debatable. According to some researchers, "What may be the stronger influence depressing performance is the poverty of many students rather than any limitations imposed by type of location" (Stern, 1994, p. 57). Some have found that both location and socioeconomic status are to blame. Researchers such as Haller and Virkler (1993) have examined the differences in student aspirations between rural and nonrural students and have found that approximately half of the difference can be attributed to the lower socioeconomic status of rural families and the other half to location.

THE STUDY

The study reported here is a 4-year investigation of the process of forming postsecondary aspirations across four ethnic groups—Asian, Latino, African American, and White. As of this writing, we are following the class of 2001 in two California high schools—one urban and one rural—with ethnically diverse populations. The fundamental questions that we are asking are as follows: How do these different groups of students come to form their postsecondary aspirations in the context of the same school environment? What is the relative role of parents, peers, and others in shaping the students' emerging aspirations? What does this process look like developmentally? We also are asking how this process differs by rural and urban contexts: What are the relative influences on rural versus urban students when analyzed by ethnicity? In this article, we report on early findings from an ongoing study with a focus on the differences between rural and urban students from two ethnic groups—White and Latino (see Table 1). We limit our analyses to these two groups because they are represented in large numbers at both school sites, whereas Asian and African American students are found in substantial numbers only at the urban high school.

Method

This study incorporates both quantitative and qualitative methods. Beginning in the fall of 1997, each year we surveyed all members of the class of 2001 in the two high schools. We asked about their attitudes toward school, future plans, and the sources

TABLE 1
Sample Sizes Split by Grade Level, School, and Ethnicity

Grade Level	Rural		Urban	
	Latino	White	Latino	White
9th grade	45	113	67	94
10th grade	41	140	82	98
11th grade	49	101	65	67

of influence on their developing identities as students, as well as their post-high-school plans. The surveys were constructed to collect longitudinal data, as well as to incorporate questions that target emerging issues, such as the onset of taking a job or acquiring a driver's license as students become older. One limitation of the study was that the sample size was not stable over time. We did not have substantial changes in the number of students at each grade level. However some fluctuations did occur in the number of students surveyed each year. This was due to the fact that we surveyed within classrooms, and therefore we captured the number of students who were in the classroom on a particular day.[1] It is also important to point out that it was not possible to link students to surveys due to concerns of anonymity. After analyzing the survey results, focus groups were held three or four times a year to interpret the data derived from the questionnaires. Focus groups were conducted with students selected to be representative of the school with respect to ethnicity and academic achievement. Extensive observation also was conducted in the schools, and in classrooms, to understand the differing contexts from which the data emerge. Currently, researchers are on site in one school daily and in the other school approximately weekly, conducting informal observation. At the beginning of the project, more formal observation, including the mapping of the school grounds with respect to student clustering, was conducted. Finally, annual data on students' grades were collected for 80 Latino and White students since the eighth grade. The sample size of 80 reflects the number of students who gave permission for their records to be released with their names and grade point averages (GPAs) and who opted to participate in the focus groups. The study is currently in its third year and will be completed in 2001.

Sites

Urban High School.   Urban High School is located about 2 miles southeast of the downtown center of a medium-sized northern California city. The school is in a residential neighborhood comprising working-class, single-family homes. Urban High School is a magnet performing arts school that draws students from all over the city, but most of the students who attend this school come from within a 5-mile radius and are of lower income and working-class origins. About 40% of the students are designated eligible for the free or reduced-price lunch program. Ap-

---

[1]Because instructional time was highly valued at both campuses, school principals left our access to classroom time for the purpose of conducting surveys to the discretion of the English departments. Faculty agreed to allow us 30 min of classroom time on 1 day only to conduct surveys. To have pressed beyond this limit to return on additional days or to pull students out of class would have violated the agreement we had with the schools and placed the data collection in jeopardy. Therefore we avoided Fridays and other days that were likely to result in lower attendance, but were not able to survey students who were absent on the survey day unless they were a part of the focus groups.

proximately 2,000 students attend the school, and the ethnic breakdown is very nearly one quarter each of Asian, African American, White, and Latino students. Most of the Latino students trace their roots to Mexico and tend to be second-generation, born in the United States. Unlike the students of color, a substantial percentage of the White students come from middle- and upper middle-class families and live outside the immediate area of the school. These students tend to be attracted to the performing arts program that is also disproportionately White. The primary staff and administration of the school are almost entirely minority, and mostly African American.

The school is the oldest in the district; however, its core buildings have been remodeled, adding substantially to its performing arts facilities, thus the campus has a relatively modern look and is reasonably well maintained. As the school population has increased, it has required that the majority of classes be held in portable trailers that take up large portions of the campus area. The school is orderly, but the hustle and bustle of 2,000 students through the relatively cramped quarters of the school site result in high noise levels and congestion during passing periods and breaks. Urban High School reports a very low dropout rate, between .5% in the 9th grade and 2.6% in the 12th grade. These figures may obscure more than they reveal, however, and may be a function of the way the district counts dropouts. For example, we noticed an almost 50% drop in the number of some students of color from the 9th to the 10th grade. When we inquired what had happened to these students, we were told that there had been a number of "transfers" of students to alternative high schools. This is usually because students are having severe academic or behavioral difficulties. Nonetheless, this very large loss of students is not counted as dropping out because students were enrolled elsewhere, at least temporarily.

Rural High School.   Rural High School is approximately a 30-min drive from Urban High School, but it might just as well be in another country. It is located in the center of an agricultural community, the only high school in this rural community with a population of less than 15,000. It serves fewer than 1,000 students in Grades 9 through 12. The student population of Rural High School is slightly more than half White, and slightly more than 40% Latino, with very small numbers of several other ethnic groups representing the balance. Almost all Latino students are of Mexican origin, and most come from families who work in the fields and in related agricultural labor; many are immigrants. The White population is somewhat more socioeconomically diverse than the Latino population, although most families are tied to the local agricultural economy. Because of its proximity to a university and a major city, some higher income White families have chosen to live in this community for lifestyle reasons, and because they have perceived it to be a good environment to rear children. Approximately one third of the students at Rural High School are on the free or reduced-price lunch program.

Although the school does not maintain statistics by ethnicity with respect to which students are served by the free lunch program, it is widely acknowledged that poverty is disproportionately a problem of the Latino population. The disproportionately high levels of poverty among Latinos are fairly typical for rural California schools (Betts et al., 2000).

Rural High School was built in the 1930s and, although old, is kept in good repair. The principal and other staff at Rural High School are mostly White. Most classes are held in permanent buildings that are located in rows behind the main campus building. The school boasts two gymnasiums, perhaps a testament to the central importance of athletics in the community. The school is very orderly and exudes a sense of safety and calm. There are several gathering places for students on the campus, and the relatively small size of the student body results in noticeably less congestion and noise than can be seen at Urban High School. Consistent with previous research, Rural High School reports a much higher dropout rate than Urban High School. It has ranged between 5% and 10% per year over the last several years. As with the free lunch program, the school does not report dropout rates by ethnicity; however, it is widely acknowledged in the community that, like poverty, dropping out is a problem endemic to Latino students. With only one high school in the district, Rural High School cannot contend that students who leave the school before graduation have transferred to alternative placements, as does Urban High School. Hence, it is not altogether clear if there are significant and real differences between the two schools with respect to dropout rates, or if there are simply fewer alternative ways to count students who leave Rural High School before graduating.

Findings

Overall developmental trends for urban and rural high school students.

The results in this section relate to both the urban and rural high schools. A repeated-measures analysis of variance (ANOVA) with GPA serving as the dependent variable showed a significant decline in GPA since the beginning of high school, $F(2, 150) = 35.91, p < .0001$. However, a chi-square test shows a significant increase in aspirations, $\chi^2(1, N = 80) = 5.128, p = .0231$ (see Figure 1).

Many students began high school without a clear idea of what they would be doing 4 years hence. Students who lived in communities where people talked about going to college or who had parents or siblings who had gone to college were more likely to report that they, too, would go to college when answering this question on the annual survey. However, 4 years can seem an eternity to a 14-year-old, and students clearly had not thought this issue through very carefully. Each year, as students became more exposed to the idea of college and postsecondary opportunities, higher proportions of students claimed they would go to college after

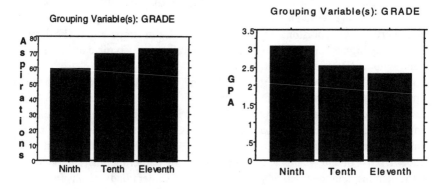

FIGURE 1   Comparison of college aspirations versus GPA for students progressing from 9th through 11th grade.

graduating from high school. However, at the same time, as a group, their grades were slipping. When this was pointed out to students—that their increasing aspirations were inconsistent with their declining grades—they suggested that they would "have to start getting serious about grades." As of 11th grade, however, they had not. High school students, even at the beginning of 11th grade, see graduation as an event that lies far into the future. They are convinced that there is still time to remedy the grade situation. Of course, most students have not considered that applications to colleges will be due in the fall of their senior year, so there is very little time left to change their GPAs. During the first 2 years of the study, Rural High School was served by two counselors. This represents a relatively low student–counselor ratio in California, where a typical urban high school with more than 2,000 students can count on no more than three counselors to serve the entire population of students.[2] Even with the smaller ratio at Rural High School, the counseling burden was simply too large for most students to spend time with a counselor considering post-high-school plans. Counselors reported that most of their time was spent arranging and rearranging students' schedules. Moreover, there has been a noticeable reluctance among Latino students in particular to consult with these counselors. Both students and counselors commented on this. In focus groups, Latino students mentioned that they did not feel comfortable with the counselors who were both White and monolingual English speakers. In the third year of the study, the school pooled its resources to hire a third counselor, a bilin-

[2]P. McDonough (personal communication, May 5, 2000) of UCLA has conducted analyses of several data sets to estimate the student–counselor ratio in California, as the state does not report these data. McDonough has not published these estimates.

gual, Latino man. The White counselors reported that, as a result, Latino student visits to the counseling office had increased.

All students are more vulnerable to peer opinion in the early years of high school. Students' responses to questions about the amount of pressure they felt to engage in "risky behaviors" (i.e., drugs, alcohol, sex, gangs) were assigned a rank from 1 (*no pressure*) to 3 (*a lot of pressure*). The results of a Kruskal–Wallis test indicate that there was a significant main effect of grade level on the amount of pressure students reported feeling to engage in risky behaviors ($H = 24.123, p < .0001$). The greatest amount of pressure was felt in the ninth grade. This decreased each year thereafter (see Table 2).

In focus groups, students explained the higher ratings for peer pressure to engage in risky behaviors in the ninth grade by saying that they were anxious to make friends and be accepted. When they first started high school this anxiety resulted in their "doing things [they] would not do now." It was clear from the focus groups that students felt very vulnerable in the first year of high school and that many experimented with behaviors that they later regretted. Once they settled on a friendship group at school, many of their anxieties began to subside and students talked of feeling "established."

There were substantial differences among ethnic groups and by gender, however, with respect to the behaviors in which they engaged. Boys were significantly more likely than girls to report pressure to use drugs and alcohol, and Latino urban boys were much more likely to report pressure to join gangs than were rural boys. In focus groups, Latina girls reported that there were stronger prohibitions against sexual activity in their community for young women, so this was a pressure that they were more likely to withstand than other girls, both out of fear of transgressing cultural norms and because they were afforded fewer opportunities to be in unsupervised settings.

Urban versus rural trends.   A number of behaviors and attitudes were significantly different for students depending on whether they were going to school in rural or urban settings. Students were asked to rank how well they got along with their parents on a 4-point scale from 1 (*very well*) to 4 (*not well at all*). To our surprise, at each grade level, rural students reported significantly less satisfactory relationships

TABLE 2
Mean Ranks for Pressure to Engage in Risky Behaviors

Grade Level	N	M Rank
9th grade	318	512.30
10th grade	360	506.65
11th grade	282	412.86

with parents, 9th grade: $t(306) = 4.735$, $p < .0001$; 10th grade: $t(350) = 3.455$, $p = .006$; 11th grade: $t(262) = 2.35$, $p = .02$ (see Table 3). Focus group discussions yielded the impression that most students were referring to the day-to-day ability to get along with their parents rather than a deep-seated rift between the generations. Students complained most about issues of control and parental concerns about the students' friends. Also in the 11th grade, students were less likely to spend time with family than with friends, $\chi^2(2, N = 262) = 6.89$, $p = .032$ (see Table 4).

Perhaps because of the stereotypes we held, we had anticipated that rural students would be more likely to spend time with parents and family and therefore would have closer family relations than urban students, who we perceived to be more tempted by urban distractions. However, rural students reported that their parents tended to be more traditional and to have expectations of their children that were more likely to conflict with the students' peer culture. Thus, these young people were struggling more to establish a sense of autonomy, which resulted in more strained parental relationships. Because relationships were more strained in the family, students contended that they sought out peers for companionship and social support more often than their urban counterparts.

Eleventh-grade students' perceptions of self and how they wanted to be viewed by their peers was another area in which urban and rural students were significantly divided. In fact, the effect of location was so strong that it appears to overwhelm ethnicity in some cases. Student surveys provided four options to the question, "How would you like other students to see you?" The first option was as a good student who helps others with their work, the second was as someone who

TABLE 3
Means and Standard Deviations for "How Well Do You Get Along With Your Parents?"

	9th Grade		10th Grade		11th Grade	
	Rural	*Urban*	*Rural*	*Urban*	*Rural*	*Urban*
n	150	156	174	176	149	113
M	2.79	3.32	2.85	3.19	3.1	3.4
SD	.69	.57	.98	.87	.54	.51

TABLE 4
Percentage of Students Choosing to Spend Free Time With Family or Friends in Eleventh Grade

	Friend	*Family*	*Other*
Rural (%)	37	3	60
Urban (%)	26	11	63

is funny and fun to be around, the third was as someone who is good looking and gets invited to all the best parties, and the fourth was as someone who is a good friend and who will always listen to others' problems. We tapped four areas that both the literature and our research show are key dimensions of adolescent self-concept. We were, however, surprised to find the degree to which urbanicity was associated with student attitudes, above and beyond ethnic affiliation.

Several things are notable in Table 5. Relatively few students wanted to be known as a good student, even if it carried the connotation of helping others with their work. Only urban Latinas rated being a good student as a persona with which they wanted to be associated in very large numbers. This is somewhat surprising, because their grades did not tend to reflect this. Only urban White students reported wanting to be viewed as someone who is good looking and who is invited to all the best parties. None of the other categories of students rated this highly. It appears that this persona is a largely urban White phenomenon. However, regardless of ethnicity, rural students tended to be more like each other than they were like their urban counterparts. For example, rural boys, whether Latino or White, overwhelmingly chose to be seen as someone who is fun to be around, and rural girls, independent of ethnicity, were most likely to want to be seen as a good friend who listens to others' problems. Urban students overall showed greater diversity in their responses than did rural students. Students' responses suggest very strongly that going to school in a rural area may have a strong homogenizing effect on their idealized high school personas—especially for boys.

Another surprising finding was that, at each grade level, rural students reported spending more time on homework than did urban students, 9th grade: χ^2 (3, $N = 310$) $= 25.662$, $p < .0001$; 10th grade: $\chi^2(3, N = 345) = 24.727$, $p < .0001$; 11th grade: $\chi^2(3, N = 282 = 46.643$, $p < .0001$. Students were asked to indicate how much time they spent on a typical evening doing homework. The options provided extended from less than 30 min to 4 or more hr. The proportion of time indicated at each grade level by rural and urban students is shown in Table 6.

The mean amount of time devoted to homework on a daily basis was 1 to 2 hr for the rural students versus 30 min to 1 hr for the urban students. However, there was no significant difference in grades between rural and urban students in spite of the different reported amounts of time spent doing homework. Moreover, the modal amount of homework that teachers of academic subjects reported assigning nightly was the same in both schools: 30 min per class. However, at Rural High School, teachers were more explicit in noting that they assigned more homework for their college-preparatory classes than for non-college-preparatory classes. This usually resulted in about 15 min more homework per night for each class. Further complicating this finding was the fact that urban students reported that grades were more important to them than did rural students. Taken together, these findings are somewhat paradoxical, but suggest that expectations may be different in the two schools, at least for some students.

TABLE 5
Students' Responses to "How Would You Like Others to See You?" by Percentages

	Latinos				Anglos			
	Urban		Rural		Urban		Rural	
	Boys (n = 23)	Girls (n = 32)	Boys (n = 28)	Girls (n = 21)	Boys (n = 26)	Girls (n = 31)	Boys (n = 47)	Girls (n = 54)
Good student (%)	12.5	41	0	5	10	4	7	27
Fun or funny (%)	34	14	79	26	47	44	71	23
Good-looking (%)	0	4.5	0	5	40	52	8	0
Good friend (%)	53	41	21	63	3	0	13	50

A chi-square test revealed that there was a significant association between aspirations of students in the 11th grade and school (rural, urban) attended, $\chi^2(3, N = 282) = 8.227, p = .04$. Consistent with other studies, the rural students in our sample were less likely to aspire to go to college and more likely to plan on going to work or into a trade after high school (see Table 7).

Although this finding is consistent with other studies, it does point to the particular influence of the rural environment as opposed to the effects of income. Rural High School actually reported a significantly lower percentage of students on free or reduced-price lunch than Urban High School. However, Rural High School proudly advertised its trade and vocational programs, including cabinet making, keyboard technology, agricultural science, and mechanics. The school also offered a number of extracurricular activities for students interested in agriculture. On the other hand, it also offered honors and advanced placement classes in six subjects, including chemistry, physics, and calculus. In focus groups, however, many students revealed that they intended to engage in occupations that their family members had pursued, and so agriculture and the trades remained attractive postsecondary options for many of these students. Evidence for this was found in the fact that, up to the 11th grade, Rural High School girls reported that their parents had a greater influence on their postsecondary decisions than did Urban High School students, $t(77) = 3.035, p = .0033$. We found this somewhat paradoxical because they also reported that they spent less time with their parents than did the urban girls (see Table 8).

TABLE 6
Amount of Time Spent on Homework on Average School Night at Each Grade

	9th Grade		10th Grade		11th Grade	
	Rural	*Urban*	*Rural*	*Urban*	*Rural*	*Urban*
<1 hr (%)	44	54	40	52	39	52
1–2 hr (%)	33	26	37	28	36	24
2–3 hr (%)	20	12	18	8	24	25
>3 hr (%)	4	8	6	10	1	3

TABLE 7
Students' Aspirations in Eleventh Grade

	2-Year College	*4-Year College*	*Job/Trade*	*Don't Know*	*Other*
Rural[a] (%)	22	46	15	10	7
Urban[b] (%)	18	57	8	8	9

[a]$n = 150.$ [b]$n = 132.$

TABLE 8
Means and Standard Deviations for 11th-Grade Girls' Rating of Parental Influence

School	n	M	SD
Rural	47	3.13	.88
Urban	30	2.50	.90

There also appear to be significant differences in the experiences of White and Latino students between Urban High School and Rural High School with respect to issues of race. At Urban High School, Latinos spoke about the racial and ethnic divisions in the school and how people tended to cluster according to their ethnicity. They also spoke of how they were made to feel inferior to both the White and Asian students by the way that activities and opportunities were structured at their school. Latino students were keenly aware that they were seldom found in the honors classes or in the coveted positions of prestige on campus. White students also acknowledged these divisions and hierarchies. However, at Rural High School, White students claimed that there were no divisions in the school and that "everyone is treated the same." However, Latinos did not agree with this claim and mentioned that there was definitely a hierarchy in the school and the White students were on the top of that hierarchy. White students were more likely to hold important roles on campus, such as cheerleader or school officer, and Latino students commented that being on the football team (which was more often the purview of the White students) was held in higher esteem than being on the soccer team (the primarily Latino sport). The differential attribution of status according to roles that are more commonly held by one group than another almost certainly sends messages to students about their perceived status in the community.

On another note, White rural girls reported feeling that they were provided more support at home than did White urban girls. By 11th grade, they saw parents as significantly, $t(77) = 3.035$, $p = .0033$, more influential than did urban White girls and they were more likely to be influenced by their teachers. Because the average income of White students' families was highest for all groups in both settings, we suspect that this was not strongly influenced by socioeconomic status. This suggests that as the girls get older, the rural context may provide more of a protective cocoon for these young women.

CONCLUSIONS

Our data suggest that there are very real differences in the ways that students experience schooling in urban versus rural environments over time. Rural students were less likely to feel pressure to engage in gang activity, more likely to report they were influenced by their parents in making important postsecondary decisions, and spent more time doing homework, but they tended to have lower aspirations to go on to college and reported more difficulty with parental relationships. They also spent less time at home with parents and family members. Thus, the news is neither all good nor all bad about going to school in this rural community. However, there are some findings that are difficult to explain.

One troubling finding is that White students in both schools were more likely to play down the extent to which racial and ethnic divisions existed in the schools and simply did not seem to see what the students of color experienced. In both Rural High School and Urban High School, Latino students noted that there were major distinctions made by students, faculty, and staff between the groups and that the Latinos consistently felt they were not held in as high esteem as the White students. Whether this was the case or not is probably not as important as the fact that the students held this perception. Importantly, however, students of color at Urban High School openly articulated these concerns. At Rural High School these feelings were swept under the rug. One cannot help but wonder if the different responses to these feelings were influenced in any way by the fact that Urban High School had an administration composed entirely of individuals of color and the school was very multiracial, whereas Rural High School's administration was all White and the school was composed of only two major ethnic groups.

The ethos at the rural school was that these things were not discussed. We found this particularly interesting because the school had made a major investment (and taken a considerable risk) in supporting an annual retreat conducted by expert consultants to address issues of difference among students. This was a highly emotional and intense day-long event in which students were strongly encouraged to voice their feelings and build bonds across ethnic groups. Students reported feeling very strongly affected by this experience. Nonetheless, as the year progressed, they tended to return to their "normal" modes of relating, clustering by ethnic group, and resuming their hierarchical positions in the school society. Evidently, an annual activity, no matter how powerful at the time, could not effectively change attitudes and behavior over the long term.

Second, although the urban high school setting appears to present greater risks for students on a number of levels—classrooms are more chaotic, students are more overtly contentious, and gang violence is a very real risk for many students—rural students run a serious risk of curtailing their aspirations, perhaps prematurely. More than one fourth of Latinas in the ninth grade had no idea what they would do after high school. This is especially troubling given the propensity for Latino students to drop out of school early. It is hard to imagine why a student would stay in high school for 4 years if it were not perceived to be a stepping stone to the next stage of life. Fortunately, this situation improves with time, but our data do not show to what extent this is a function of students becoming more acquainted with their options, or of students who hold low aspirations dropping out. The apparent impact of the rural school environment in shaping students' idealized personas was also notable. Whereas urban students had more diverse responses to how they would like others to see them, rural students, and especially boys, defined themselves much more narrowly, and few saw being a good student as particularly desirable.

Of course, there is a certain arrogance in our assumptions as well. Some students were following in their parents' footsteps in working the land or entering the trades as they described their futures. These choices were heavily tied to the expectations of their families. It is thus difficult to conclude that these students made choices out of ignorance, or that another choice—like college—would be better for them. However, the extent to which these noncollege options are exercised more often by lower income students, and by children of immigrants with little education themselves, raises the specter of inequality and compels us to question the role of the schools in equalizing opportunity.

Across both schools, we are impressed with the fact that many students seemed to believe that high school would last forever and that it was never too late to turn things around in preparing for college or for other postsecondary options. Even though aspirations were higher at Urban High School, students in both schools believed, into the 11th grade, that there was still plenty of time to change course. This is a relatively common feature of adolescence, but little attention has been paid to adolescents' conceptions of time in the research literature. We think it deserves more attention. For adolescents, 4 years is roughly a quarter of their lives, and so it seems an extraordinarily long period of time. It might be difficult for most adults to conceive of time in the same way these adolescents do, and therefore to understand why many students do not respond to adult concerns about preparing for the time after high school. Students whose parents have the social and cultural capital to aid their children in successfully transitioning to postsecondary opportunities can buffer this perceptual difference for their children. They help them to set higher personal standards and provide the kinds of experiences that keep them on track and in the college pipeline. Parents with less social and cultural capital are not able to provide this kind of backup for their children, who will wait until the last moment of high school to find that it is too late to change course and that many opportunities have been foreclosed.

Finally, we are challenged by the finding that students at Rural High School contended that they spent less time with their parents and family and felt that these relations were more stressful, yet they also reported that their parents had a greater influence on their future plans. Of course, it is also somewhat ironic that the rural students, in expressing that their parents had a greater influence on their long-term decisions, also had less ambition to go to college. Presumably, the urban students were getting the message to go to college from some place other than home, although they did not report being more influenced by teachers, friends, or media than the rural students.

The literature is consistent in finding that students with strong parental relations are less likely to engage in risky behaviors and more likely to make healthy behavioral choices (Resnick et al., 1997). The inference that can be made from these findings is that students with good family relations are more likely to listen to the advice and guidance that their parents provide. It is therefore difficult to reconcile the finding that rural students reported less satisfactory relationships with parents but sensed more parental influence. We speculate that this is related to different social patterns in rural communities that are not well explained by existing research. As our study reaches completion, we hope to shed more light on this, and other conundrums, raised by our data.

ACKNOWLEDGMENTS

This work was supported under the Education Research and Development Program (PR/Award R306A60001), the Center for Research on Education, Diversity and Excellence, as administered by the Office of Educational Research and Improvement (OERI), National Institute on the Education of At-Risk Students (NIEARS), and the U.S. Department of Education (USDOE).

The contents, findings, and opinions expressed in this article are those of the authors and do not necessarily represent the positions or policies of OERI, NIEARS, or the USDOE.

REFERENCES

Ballou, D., & Podgursky, M. (1995). Rural schools: Fewer highly trained teachers and special programs, but better learning environment. *Rural Development Perspectives, 10,* 6–16.

Betts, J., Rueben, K., & Danenberg, A. (2000). *Equal resources, equal outcomes? The distribution of school resources and student achievement in California.* San Francisco: Public Policy Institute of California.

Brown, B., & Theobald, W. (1998). Learning contexts beyond the classroom: Extracurricular activities, community organizations, and peer groups. In K. Borman & B. Schneider (Eds.), *The adolescent years: Social influences and educational challenges. 97th year book for the National Society for the Study of Education. Part I* (pp. 109–141). Chicago: University of Chicago Press.

Carmichael, D. (1982). The challenge of rural education. *Rural Educator, 3,* 5–10.

Carnegie Council on Adolescent Development. (1995). *Great transitions: Preparing adolescents for a new century.* New York: Carnegie Corporation.

Cooper, C., & Cooper, R. (1992). Links between adolescents' relationships with their parents and peers: Models, evidence, and mechanisms. In R. Parke & G. Ladd (Eds.), *Family peer relationships: Models of linkages* (pp. 135–158). Hillsdale, NJ: Lawrence Erlbaum Associates, Inc.

Cooper, C. R., Jackson, J. F., Azmitia, M., Lopez, E. M., & Dunbar, N. (1995). Bridging students' multiple worlds: African American and Latino youth in academic outreach programs. In R. F. Macías & R. G. García Ramos (Eds.), *Changing schools for changing students: An anthology of research on language minorities* (pp. 211–234). Santa Barbara: University of California Linguistic Minority Research Institute.

Csikszentmihalyi, M., & Schmidt, J. (1998). Stress and resilience in adolescence: An evolutionary perspective. In K. Borman & B. Schneider (Eds.), *The adolescent years: Social influences and educational challenges. 97th year book for the National Society for the Study of Education. Part I* (pp. 1–17). Chicago: University of Chicago Press.

DeYoung, A. (1992). *At-risk children and the reform of rural schools: Economic and cultural dimensions.* Palo Alto, CA: American Institutes for Research in the Behavioral Sciences. (ERIC Document Reproduction Service No. ED 361 153)

Eccles, J., Midgely, C., Wigfield, A., Buchanan, C., Reuman, D., Flanagan, C., & MacIver, D. (1993). Development during adolescence. The impact of stage-environmental fit on young adolescents' experiences in schools and in families. *American Psychologist, 48,* 90–101.

Erikson, E. (1968). *Identity, youth, and crisis.* New York: Norton.

Foley, D. (1990). *Learning capitalist culture: Deep in the heart of Tejas.* Philadelphia: University of Pennsylvania.

Fordham, S., & Ogbu, J. (1986). Black students' school success: Coping with the burden of "acting White." *Urban Review, 18,* 176–206.

Gándara, P. (1995). *Over the ivy walls: The educational mobility of low income Chicanos.* Albany: State University of New York Press.

Grotevant, H. D., & Cooper, C. R. (1985). Patterns of interaction in family relationships and the development of identity formation in adolescence. *Child Development, 56,* 415–428.

Haller, E., & Virkler, S. (1993). Another look at rural–nonrural differences in students' educational aspirations. *Journal of Research in Rural Education, 9,* 170–178.

Kao, G., & Tienda, M. (1998). Educational aspirations of minority youth. *American Journal of Education, 106,* 349–384.

Khattri, N., Riley, K. W., & Kane, M. B. (1997). Students at risk in poor, rural areas: A review of the research. *Research in Rural Education, 13,* 79–100.

Kimmel, E., & Rudolph, T. (1998). Growing up female. In K. Borman & B. Schneider (Eds.), *The adolescent years: Social influences and educational challenges. 97th year book for the National Society for the Study of Education. Part I* (pp. 42–64). Chicago: University of Chicago Press.

Marcia, J. (1980). Ego identity development. In J. Adelson (Ed.), *The handbook of adolescent psychology* (pp. 159–187). New York: Wiley.

Markus, H., & Nurius, P. (1986). Possible selves. *American Psychologist, 41,* 954–969.

Matute-Bianchi, E. (1986). Ethnic identities and patterns of school success and failure among Mexican-descent and Japanese American students in a California high school: An ethnographic analysis. *American Journal of Education, 95,* 233–255.

National Center for Education Statistics. (1999). *Digest of education statistics.* Washington, DC: U.S. Government Printing Office.

National Research Council. (1993). *Losing generations: Adolescents in high-risk settings.* Washington, DC: National Research Council Panel on High Risk Youth, National Academy of Sciences.

Phelan, P., Davidson, A., & Cao, H. (1991). Students' multiple worlds: Negotiating the boundaries of family, peer, and school cultures, *Anthropology and Education Quarterly, 22,* 224–250.

Resnick, M., Bearman, P., Blum, R., Bauman, K., Harris, K., Jones, J., Tabor, J., Beuhring, T., Sieving, R., Shew, M., Ireland, M., Bearinger, L., & Udry, R. (1997). Protecting adolescents from harm: Findings from the National Longitudinal Study of Adolescent Health. *Journal of the American Medical Association, 278,* 823–832.

Sadker, M., & Sadker, D. (1994). *Failing at fairness: How America's schools cheat girls.* New York: Scribner.

Sherman, A. (1992). *Falling on the wayside: Children in rural America.* Washington, DC: Children's Defense Fund.

Stanton-Salazar, R. (in press). *Perilous webs: The social support networks and help-seeking experiences of working- class Mexican-origin adolescents.* Albany: State University of New York Press.

Steinberg, L. (1996). *Beyond the classroom.* New York: Simon & Schuster.

Steinberg, L., Brown, B., Cider, M., Kaczmarek, N., & Lazzaro, C. (1988). *Non-instructional influences on high school student achievement: The contributions of parents, peers, extracurricular activities, and part time work.* Madison: National Center on Effective Secondary Schools, University of Wisconsin, Wisconsin Center for Education Research.

Steinberg, L., Dornbusch, S., & Brown, B. (1992). Ethnic differences in adolescent achievement. *American Psychologist, 47,* 723–729.

Stern, J. D. (1994). *The condition of education in rural schools.* Washington, DC: Office of Educational Research and Improvement. (ERIC Document Reproduction Service No. ED 371 935)

Swanson, D., Spencer, M., & Petersen, A. (1998). Identity formation in adolescence. In K. Borman & B. Schneider (Eds.), *The adolescent years: Social influences and educational challenges. 97th year book for the National Society for the Study of Education. Part I* (pp. 18–41). Chicago: University of Chicago Press.

JOURNAL OF EDUCATION FOR STUDENTS PLACED AT RISK, 6(1&2), 95–113

Latino Immigrant Parents and Children Learning and Publishing Together in an After-School Setting

Richard Durán, Jane Durán, Deborah Perry-Romero, and
Edith Sanchez

Graduate School of Education
University of California, Santa Barbara

In this article, we overview 1 year's activities of an after-school project convening immigrant, low-income Latino parents and elementary schoolchildren for the purpose of learning and publishing together. The intent of the project is to help parents acquire a working familiarity with computers and computer-related technologies as tools for learning and communication in collaboration with their children. We describe the evolution and design of the project into a community-based learning community involving the family, teachers, university staff, and community members. We also present a description of computer learning and publishing activities. We then summarize data showing parents' growth in computer skills. In addition, qualitative research findings on parents' and children's interaction are provided with connections to sociocultural theory. In the concluding section we give attention to a cultural-historical theoretical account of the learning community and implications for thinking about the ways in which new technologies are mediating learning and schooling for immigrant families.

THE DIGITAL DIVIDE, SCHOOLING, AND IMMIGRANT LATINO FAMILIES

A great deal of public policy attention is being given to the existence of a digital divide in access to computers and related technology among the poor and certain ethnic racial minorities and more affluent groups (National Telecommunications and

Requests for reprints should be sent to Richard Durán, Graduate School of Education, University of California, Santa Barbara, Santa Barbara, CA 93106. E-mail: duran@education.ucsb.edu

Information Administration, 1999). The situation is quite dynamic. Recent National Center for Education Statistics (NCES, 2000) data show that by 1999, 95% of schools in the United States had access to both computers and the Internet, a rapid rise from 35% since 1995. However, other NCES data emerging from the National Assessment of Educational Progress (NAEP) suggest that within schools, the use of computers and technology varies noticeably among ethnic minority racial groups. Data from the NAEP Reading Achievement survey indicate that Hispanic students are more likely to use computers for remedial learning tasks than White nonminority students.

The emergence of computer technology and computer-aided communications in everyday life and schools has consequences that are not well understood for devising ways to improve educational outcomes among low-income immigrant families. On the one hand, technology and the digital divide between access to technology among the "haves" and "have-nots" represent a barrier for improving educational outcomes among Latino immigrant students. We cannot expect Latino students to learn more and more effectively when they do not have the same access to computers as other children, and when they do not have the same opportunities to learn when using computers at schools as children from more affluent backgrounds.

However, there are other possibilities that are beginning to be explored, which might begin to exploit the availability of technology toward radically reframing and improving the learning opportunities of Latino immigrant students. Constructing new kinds of learning environments utilizing computers and related technology outside of schools represents one such reframing that deserves close examination and research.

THE PROJECT

Involving parents in their children's education has long been recognized as a significant factor in contributing to student success. Qualitative research with low-income Latino families supports this conclusion and indicates that children learn well when their parents are actively involved in their learning (Delgado-Gaitan, 1990; Delgado-Gaitan & Trueba, 1991; Goldenberg, 1987). However, before we can effectively measure the consequences of parental involvement, it is important to establish effective means for encouraging parents of children, especially of those most at risk, to participate in their children's education. Beyond this, we need to create social contexts for joint learning that are enduring and able to empower the interaction of parents, children, and collaborating facilitators in promoting joint learning. It is valuable to consider locations in the community outside homes as an important resource for such an endeavor. This is especially useful for families that are not likely to have computers at home. It is also useful if a venue is available where many computers and associated technology are located, and if it can be coupled with availability of persons to help familiarize parents with the use of computers as well as for guiding their use for learning. An added dimension is that research has found that Latino immigrant families may benefit from efforts by community members and school personnel who might be available to broker parents' understanding of schooling practices and expectations schools have of students (Valdes, 1996).

Our project involves the development of computer-based literacy and empowerment for low-income Latino parents and their schoolchildren. Small groups of parents have been invited to participate and interact with their children on computers. The sessions have focused on parent–child interaction regarding literacy and increased familiarity with technology. We introduced parents to basic computer awareness and hands-on experience through the creation of word processing documents and some Internet activities in collaboration with children. Parents and children worked together with facilitators, school teachers, and a university research team to produce a desktop magazine that is distributed to participants, family, and friends.

Cultural and linguistic compatibility are important components of our project. Coupled with the nature of the activities we undertake, these components have created a new kind of community-based learning setting for families and children. Our project operates like a community-based organization. It involves immigrant families and children, school teachers, and university students and faculty researchers sharing both commonalities and differences in their sociocultural experiences and language competencies. It includes participation of other community members who share their knowledge of literacy and technology with participating families and children and other team members.

Characteristics of Parents and Recruitment During 1998–1999

Our target parents are usually native speakers of Spanish. Their command of English is often limited, although a few attend English language classes. Typically, we have parents with only basic literacy skills. All of the children involved in the project are familiar with Spanish at home, but as mandated by the California education code, all children are being schooled solely in English. Accordingly, we have elected to conduct our project sessions primarily in Spanish. Although English is used less, parents, children, and other participants use English liberally in their communications, and parents and children produce work and publications in English or Spanish as they elect.

During the 1998–1999 academic year, we served a total of 24 parents and 20 children. Parents were recruited to the project with several strategies. First, Latino parents of children in the fourth- and sixth-grade classrooms of the two participating teachers were invited to attend. Second, parents of children who attend the local after-school computer venture at the Boys and Girls Club in Goleta, Club Proteo, were also invited. Third, recruitment was also carried out directly in the community via flyers and personal promotion. Several participants attended the project by word of mouth through information passed on by families and friends. Members from past years were also invited.

The backgrounds of participants were extremely diverse. Two uniting factors were that all were first-generation immigrants from Mexico and all had children in elementary Grades K through 6. Several had young infants and older children (junior high to high school age) as well. Families of participating parents ranged in size from 2 to 10 children. Questionnaire data collected indicated that fathers typically worked in manual labor jobs, such as gardening or construction, and mothers worked as hotel maids and house cleaners, and as housewives in addition to their jobs outside the home. The educational background of the adults varied considerably. Many parents had only completed elementary school in Mexico, having then been obligated to work; a small proportion completed the equivalent of high school in Mexico. Extreme cases include a young mother who admitted that she did not know how to read and write except for her name, and the contrasting case of a father who, since being with this project in the previous year, had gone on to enroll in classes at the local city college. Two of the mothers had some typing skills, but no adult female participants had ever used a computer before. Only two families had a computer at home. One family had an old Apple computer at home, and a second family acquired a used 486 computer (i.e., three generations old) after joining the project, which they asked one of our participating teachers to help them set up.

Design of Sessions, Goals, and Activities for Parents and Children

Our main aim was to focus on ways to introduce Latino parents to computer-based literacy practices that not only resembled those their children encounter at school, but also allowed for parents and children to engage in new, joint, mediated activities. We elected to focus on the production of meaningful texts. Our goals were to couple this with computer graphics, and to focus on narrative genres used at school and resonate with the cultural experiences of parents and children in the form of stories. By creating opportunities for parents and children to have access to technology beyond the classroom and by providing support from the project team, we were aiming to increase not only their awareness but also their participation in the literary practices of their school and community.

In this article we describe activities during the 1998–1999 school year. We met in two cycles over the course of the academic year (September through June 1998–1999) for approximately 2 hr per session, from 6 p.m. until 8 p.m. We met in the school computer room. Use of the school computer lab was an important factor aiding implementation of the project. This computer lab featured more than 20 recent model Macintosh computers with CD-ROM drives connected to a high-speed Internet connection via a file server. The computer room had a digital scanner and two printers, plus a large monitor linked to a computer for the purpose of group presentations.

The fall cycle of meetings lasted 10 weeks, and included a field trip to a local university. The spring cycle of meetings lasted 12 weeks. We designed sessions to fall into two multiple-week cycles. Our earlier experiences indicated that we needed to establish a reasonable participation commitment among parents and children. We needed a sufficient number of sessions to allow for learning important computer skills and to permit production of a publication. We ended the fall cycle as the Christmas holiday approached and began the spring cycle toward the end of February. The division of our meetings into two cycles permitted parents to join or leave the project easily. Parents were invited to stay with the project for both cycles and beyond, but the commitment to attend only one cycle at a time provided a comfort factor for parents and children. Allowing the parents to end their commitment after a cycle preserved their identity as meeting a commitment to the project and leaving in good graces.

During Fall 1998 we ran an initial 10-week session focusing on helping parents acquire a basic familiarity with computers, using word processing software programs, and facilitating parents' and children's production of narratives aided by computers. The meetings and the activities and learning goals of each meeting during 1998–1999 can be found in the Appendix. The fall series of sessions combined the introduction of computer activities that would enable parents and children to plan, research, and write about a legend of their choice. Responses to our initial parent questionnaire indicated that parents, overall, had no or only limited experience with computers. In contrast, many of the children of parents attending sessions had learned how to use computers at school and were familiar with the computer room being used for sessions. Thus we had to design activities that gave parents with little or no knowledge of computers a focused opportunity to learn how to use a computer, at the same time engaging their children in meaningful and satisfying activities. We sought ways for adult and child participants to share their knowledge or expertise with each other and tasks that required collaboration. For example, we would establish at the beginning of a session that the children would be responsible for reporting back to the group on the progress or discoveries made. In this way parents and children would seek each other out during the session.

Our planning and implementation of sessions required collaboration among university and school teachers. Activities were planned and implemented to help parents use computers, software, and the Internet. Our two participating teachers led the development of activities that focused on exploring legends, an area many of the children studied at school during the fall. Computer, software, and Internet learning were tied to learning objectives we had established for parents and to our pre- and postassessment for their learning. We needed to establish a set of well-defined learning objectives for parents in these areas that were targeted and articulated for learning within and across project sessions.

As parents developed familiarity with computers, we included additional activities that were designed to familiarize parents with ways in which their children were taught at school to think about writing, narrative legends, and their production. It was important to ground these additional activities and learning of basic computer skills for the purpose of sense making. Computers and electronic technology were introduced as tools for learning about culture and the world, and for being able to connect prior knowledge and experience to new knowledge and positioning of self and family understandings. The participating teachers and university team members introduced parents to school supplies such as folders, pens, notebooks, and other artifacts used by children in writing. Teachers also introduced parents to ways in which children used brainstorming and a special schema (KWLQ; What I know, what I want to know, what I have learned, and what questions I have) to organize research for a story. Children's participation in these activities was important. With help from teachers and university staff, children modeled for parents how they used these tools in producing stories that could then be written. The Fall 1999 cycle ended with parents and children jointly reading the legends they had published.

As shown in the Appendix, the design and implementation of the Spring 1999 cycle included activities designed to help parents acquire targeted computer skills and use computers to develop and publish narratives. In addition, parents and children were provided means to explore cultural understandings more deeply and opportunities to interact with community members who used computers to publish as part of their professional accomplishments.

The spring cycle included the goal of desktop publishing of autobiographical materials developed in joint activities by parents and children. The cycle featured guest presentations by Norma Cantú, the well-known Chicana author from the border region of Texas; Victor Fuentes of the University of California, Santa Barbara (UCSB), Spanish Department; the editor of the Spanish language literary journal *Ventana Abierta;* and the publishers of the local Spanish language community newspaper, *El Sol.* At each meeting, the parents heard guests' descriptions of how literacy had become empowering, and in the instance of the newspaper presenters, how computers were used in the development, editing, and publishing of the newspaper.

The theme for the parents' work during the spring cycle was development and publication of autobiographical narratives. This theme was developed by having parents and children reflect on Cantú's (1995) autobiography (*Canícula*) describing her childhood in Texas. Parents and children were able to use the Internet to visit Cantú's personal Web page and gain an understanding of how the Internet has become a medium for cultural expression and publication. Asking each parent to focus on his or her memories of childhood and young adulthood enabled the group to produce a number of documents on the computer detailing events in their lives that had meaning both for them and for other family members. These pieces were accompanied by graphic drawings or digitized photos that were compiled in a desktop publication entitled *Profundos Recuerdos* ("Profound Memories," a title of the parents' choosing). During our last session, Cantú visited again and heard parents and children read aloud from their publications.

Assessment of Parents' Learning of Computer Skills and Results

We administered pre- and postassessments for each cycle. We administered the preassessment orally. However, for the postassessment for each of these cycles, we had parents "work through" the assessment questions while seated at a computer with their children recording parents' use of the equipment. This performance assessment allowed parents to actually display their ability at the computer, rather than just affirm knowledge or familiarity in response to a purely oral questionnaire. We were able to collect completed pre- and postassessments for 18 of the parent participants. These assessment areas included:

- Computer awareness (10 questions).
- Computer basics (12 questions).
- Basic word processing skills (5 questions).
- Multimedia and telecommunications familiarity (10 questions).

Table 1 reports the results of matched pairs t tests comparing the pre- and postassessment scores of the 18 parents based on mean scores over questions in each assessment area. Inspection of these results indicates that the 18 parents showed statistically significant gains in every area of assessment over the course of their participation in the project during 1998–1999. Gains were evident for each question in each of the four areas assessed, except for two, suggesting a comprehensive improvement in skills as a result of participating in the project. Gains were most prominent and of the largest magnitude with regard to three questions probing knowledge of the Internet in the area of multimedia and telecommunications familiarity. Interestingly, parents showed no gain in knowledge in this area with regard to questions probing knowledge of how to download files from the Internet and how to use bookmarks to store Web page addresses.

TABLE 1
Results of Matched Pairs t Tests of Pre- and Postassessments by Assessment Areas
(1998–1999) (N = 18)

Area	No. of Questions	Premean: Yes Answers	SD	Postmean: Yes Answers	SD	2-Tail Significance
Computer awareness	10	4.61	5.00	9.56	3.68	.000
Computer basics	12	5.16	5.12	9.55	3.68	.000
Word processing	5	2.06	2.10	3.56	1.89	.003
Multimedia and telecommunic ations	10	1.61	2.12	4.83	3.31	.000
Total	37	15.78	11.74	27.00	9.46	.000

As shown in Table 1, the difference in pre- and postquestion means was highly significant when questions were collapsed over all areas, as would be expected given the results for each separate question area. Over the pre- and postassessment, parents went from averaging a mean of 15 of 37 total questions answered affirmatively to an average of 27 questions responded to affirmatively by demonstrating a skill on the postassessment. In terms of proportional gains, parents on the preassessment showed an average knowledge of 32% of the computer literacy skills assessed by questions. By the postassessment, this jumped to an average of 73% knowledge of the skills reflected in the questions. These results support the hypothesis that exposure to project activities helps parents acquire computer literacy skills. The results represent an encouraging first step in establishing evidence that exposure to the project benefits parents.

We did not use pre- and postassessment questionnaires with the children. There were insufficient resources available to the project to include these assessments. This is not a new problem to researchers investigating and formulating more comprehensive connections between family literacy programs and benefits to students.

The children who participated came from several different classrooms and grades. Although the narrative writing activities developed with help from participating teachers were familiar to children, they were not coordinated with current classroom activities in which the children engaged. Therefore, it was not feasible to design assessments of specific school learning outcomes for children based on project activities.

Research on Interaction During Computer Learning Sessions

Two qualitative case studies using ethnography and discourse analysis methods were conducted during 1998–1999, investigating interaction among parents and children during computer sessions. The purpose of these studies was to understand the nature of the problem solving in which parents and children engaged as they worked together on various activities in the development of narratives for desktop publication. These case studies were conducted to develop a grounded theoretical account substantiating how Sociocultural Theory might contribute to understanding the accomplishments of parents and children. Still another purpose was to understand the development and problem-solving abilities of the broader learning community of teachers and university staff constituting the learning community at hand. This research direction was developed following review of our progress and after we realized the need to shift from a "training and skills" perspective on processes and outcomes of the project toward a "learning community" account of participation and outcomes (Rogoff, Matusov, & White, 1996). We were influenced to move in this direction by a review of our project that included prominent investigators in cognitive anthropology (Evelyn Jacob) and interactional sociolinguistics (Fred Erickson). We were persuaded that close analyses of interaction among parents and children in computer learning sessions provided a unique opportunity to understand how sociocultural theory could account for the development of computer-related literacy competencies among immigrant families and children. Our move in this direction was buttressed by previous experience in discourse analysis research as applied to cognitive studies.

One case study we conducted examined the discourse practices and development of a text by an adult using a computer for the first time. We examined how both the computer room and sociocultural setting were related to the interactions that took place in the writing of the text and its content. We analyzed how the participants as writers generated their agency and identity as writers as they wrote it little by little. As the parents and children wrote together, they engaged in focused problem solving about language content (word selection for intended meaning), language organization, and language form (spelling, grammar, and punctuation) as mediated by the computer and its software. We tracked how a parent chose to focus her attention on punctuation, despite having been encouraged to revise content. We concluded that parents and children who engage in joint writing on the computer are gradually developing expertise regarding desktop publishing itself as a complex genre of activity. That is to say, parents and children began to show evidence that they knew what desktop publishing was as an activity—an activity type that was part of their ongoing repertoire for communication via a computer.

A second ethnographic case study focused on a detailed analysis of a father's and son's nonverbal interaction as they worked together in the production of a written text. The study examined the pragmatic, social aspects of their nonverbal communication and how meaning and task orientation were related to significant shifts in their physical interpersonal distance and posture over activities and events. The postural and proxemic configurations were viewed as culturally recognized and conventional signals or cues, marking boundaries among connected but separable actions (Goodwin & Goodwin, in press; Gumperz, 1981). The analyses suggest that learning interaction is constituted by both content and form of interaction, similar to a consequential progression account of learning activity (Putney et al., 1999). In other words, when people interact in joint learning activities, they are not only acquiring knowledge of what to learn but also knowledge of how to learn by means of strategic design of their interactions.

The data of the case study show how a fourth-grade boy communicated with his father while they engaged in their text production. The opportunities for communicative exchanges serving different purposes are important elements to consider when we think further about the implications of affording parents, adults, and children spaces for these types of interaction. Examples of joint mediated activity were presented and served to illustrate the coconstructed nature of mind as action (Wertsch, 1998).

The data provided an insight into the types of participation structures that operate in interaction among project participants. We saw how closely both father and son negotiated through actions their strategies for joint writing. Structures and interactions that frequently called for alternating the roles of expert and novice were evident and allowed for each participant to explore a range of dimensions of their relationship relevant to literacy and literacy practice.

We confirmed that Latino parents have much to offer their children even though they might not always be familiar with schooled literacy practices. By breaking stereotypes of expected or defined behavior within and beyond the classroom, we gained a fresh understanding of what collaboration means and how computer technology enables learning and connections to children's schooling.

CONCLUSIONS AND IMPLICATIONS

Our efforts and results thus far suggest that our after-school computer learning project for immigrant Latino parents and children has created a new form of community-based organization. This organization interconnects family members, teachers, university students and faculty, and others from the community at large. The result has been a new learning community that helps familiarize parents with the use of computers and information technology in a manner that incorporates children's knowledge of computers and information technology and literacy tasks provided at school. We found that parents with no computers at home and with little or no prior skill in the use of computers rapidly developed computer skills and became familiar with desktop publishing. Although to date our design of assessment and evaluation procedures to measure parents' computer skills learning has been rudimentary, the initial evidence is positive.

Our formula for successful implementation of the project has involved a careful blending of support for parents' learning of computer skills with sense-making literacy activities involving their children. This was connected to familiar literacy activities children encounter in schooling, and with cultural sense making more generally. Having parents and children explore development of narratives in the form of legends or autobiographical narratives was very productive. The implementation of these literacy activities was richly connected to exploration of sense making provided by community members visiting the project. The visit of Cantú to read in Spanish from her biography and to stimulate parents' and children's thoughts about the meaning and personal value of biographies was significant.

The effectiveness of this tool for the development of parent and child involvement also has an important theoretical dimension. Contemporary cultural psychology and activity theory approaches to human development and literacy emphasize ways in which narrative knowing constitutes a basic form of human cognition about the everyday world and cultural practice (see, e.g., the extensive work of Bruner, 1986, 1990, 1996; Cole, 1996; and Wertsch, 1991, 1998).

Cantú's presentation and the earlier sessions on legends inspired parents and children to think about how their lives as narrative experiences were central to literacy as represented by published and oral legends and biographies. There was no question that parents and children had a rich knowledge base on which to build their own narratives. Importantly, the presentation of legend activities and autobiography development activities emphasized the creative nature of these activities. These could then be communicated via desktop publication on a computer. Presentations to the publishers of a local Spanish language newspaper and the publisher of a Spanish language literary journal likely reinforced the perception of parents and children that communication in print via computer tools was attainable by all, and was possible in and out of school because language and thinking skills acquired in school were reflected in the real world of publishing. The ideas, emotions, and life views expressed by eminent as well as everyday persons published in the journal were about knowing and understanding the world in the profound richness of everyday experience.

The publishers of the local Spanish language newspaper added to this emphasis on the importance of literacy skills and the examination and analysis of experience. Apart from emphasizing the importance of news and celebrations of culture through the medium of a community newspaper, the publishers also gave prominent attention to ways in which computers played essential roles in the newspaper's development. They discussed and showed how the format, content, use of graphics, and the fundamental processes in editing a newspaper to meet grammatical and structural standards for publication were aided by computers. Connections to schooled literacy practices of children were made, such as how students must draft, edit, and revise their written work prior to its final presentation for discussion and evaluation. These important notions of literacy were seen to be components of everyday life and literacy. Concerns for drafting, editing, and revising were also embedded in the activities designed for parents.

The power of the computer to both draft and change text was made evident to participants as an essential tool for manifesting competency, and was built directly into the skills parents learned as they became familiar with how to operate a computer. Some parents had been initially reluctant to begin to work on the computer; however, almost all parents were able to overcome initial hesitations and go on to produce work. This was the case even with the minority of parents who lacked the basic requisite literacy skills. One woman who had never been exposed to formal schooling and hence did not know the alphabet was able to achieve completion of a small project involving a computer, a printer, and scanning equipment. She proudly exhibited her scanned and printed photograph of her family, which she produced with the assistance of a UCSB graduate student who helped her overcome her fears of the equipment. Her use of the mouse to control the shading reproduction of the scanned photograph was an indicator of the degree to which even individuals who had never had formal schooling can become familiar with at least some computer-related activities.

Activity theory (see Nardi, 1997) provides a promising lens with which to understand the complex interlacing of motoric and symbolic operations and higher level symbolic activity, framing and making possible more complex literate action made accessible by computers. Kaptelinin (1997) argued that grounded analyses of action are needed. These must take into account how basic operations on a computer represent more complex interaction with and through social and cultural means. In the present context of immigrant families and their children, the learning of computer skills by parents and children needs to be tied to more complex analyses of the forms of social, cultural, and institutional capital that they empower among family members and communities (Cummins & Sayers, 1997; Durán, 1996; Vásquez & Durán, in press). Implementation of such research utilizing tools of discourse analysis and conversation analysis remains important in current and long-term goals of this project. Thus the goals of our project must join the world of action as seen by our community of learners and the world of focused analytic investigation of data and evidence regarding the construction of this world of action among community members.

ACKNOWLEDGMENTS

This work was supported under the Education Research and Development Program (PR/Award R306A60001), the Center for Research on Education, Diversity and Excellence, as administered by the Office of Educational Research and Improvement (OERI), National Institute on the Education of At-Risk Students (NIEARS), and the U.S. Department of Education (USDOE).

The contents, findings, and opinions expressed in this article are those of the authors and do not necessarily represent the positions or policies of OERI, NIEARS, or the USDOE.

REFERENCES

Bruner, J. (1986). *Actual minds, possible worlds.* Cambridge, MA: Harvard University Press.

Bruner, J. (1990). *Acts of meaning.* Cambridge, MA: Harvard University Press.

Bruner, J. (1996). *The culture of education.* Cambridge, MA: Harvard University Press.

Cantú, N. (1995). *Canícula: Snapshots of a girlhood en la frontera.* Albuquerque: University of New Mexico Press.

Cole, M. (1996). *Cultural psychology.* Cambridge, MA: Harvard University Press.

Cummins, J., & Sayers, D. (1997). *Brave new schools: Challenging cultural illiteracy through global learning networks.* Cambridge, MA: Harvard University Press.

Delgado-Gaitan, C. (1990). *Literacy for empowerment: The role of parents in children's education.* Bristol, PA: Falmer.

Delgado-Gaitan, C., & Trueba, H. (1991). *Crossing cultural borders: Education for immigrant families in America.* London: Falmer.

Durán, R. P. (1996). English immigrant language learners: Cultural accommodations and family literacy. In L. Benjamin & J. Lord (Eds.), *Family literacy: Directions in research and implications for practice.* Washington, DC: U.S. Department of Education, Office of Educational Research and Improvement.

Goldenberg, C. (1987). Low-income Hispanic parents' contributions to their first-grade children's word-recognition skills. *Anthropology and Education Quarterly, 18,* 149–179.

Goodwin, C., & Goodwin, M. H. (in press). Formulating planes: Seeing as a situated activity. In D. Middleton & Y. Engestrom (Eds.), *Cognition and communication at work.* Cambridge, England: Cambridge University Press.

Gumperz, J. (1981). *Discourse strategies.* Cambridge, England: Cambridge University Press.

Kaptelinin, V. (1997). Computer-mediated activity: Functional organs in social and developmental contexts. In B. Nardi (Ed.), *Context and consciousness: Activity theory and human–computer interaction. Cambridge, MA: MIT Press.*

Nardi, B. (Ed.). (1997). *Context and consciousness: Activity theory and human–computer interaction.* Cambridge, MA: MIT Press.

National Center for Education Statistics. (2000). *Stats in brief: Internet access in U.S. public schools and classrooms: 1994–99.* Washington, DC: U.S. Department of Education.

National Telecommunications and Information Administration. (1999). *Falling through the NET: Defining the digital divide.* Washington, DC: U.S. Department of Commerce.

Putney, L., Green, J., Dixon, C., Duran, R., Floriani, A., & Yeager, B. (1999). Consequential progressions: Exploring collective–individual development in a bilingual classroom. In C. Lee & P. Smagorinsky (Eds.), *Vygotskian perspectives on literacy research.* New York: Cambridge University Press.

Rogoff, B., Matusov, E., & White, C. (1996). Models of learning in a community of learners. In D. R. Olson & N. Torrance (Eds.), *Handbook of education and human development: New models of learning, teaching, and schooling.* London: Basil Blackwell.

Valdes, G. (1996). *Con respeto: Bridging the distance between culturally diverse families and schools: An ethnographic portrait.* New York: Teachers College Press.

Vásquez, O., & Durán, R. P. (in press). *La Clase Mágica* and *El Club Proteo*: Multiple literacies in new community contexts. In G. Gallego & S. Hollingsworth (Eds.), *Challenging a single standard: Perspectives on multiple literacies*. New York: Teachers College Press.

Wertsch, J. (1991). *Voices of the mind*. Cambridge, MA: Harvard University Press.

Wertsch, J. (1998). *Mind as action*. New York: Oxford University Press.

APPENDIX
OVERVIEW OF WEEKLY PLANS

Fall 1998

Week 1: Introduction and Project Presentation

1. Pretest parents on computer awareness and basics.
2. Familiarization with computer: monitor, keyboard, mouse, and so on.
3. Computer activity: Parents and children review computer and practice turning on and off.
4. Handout materials: journals, folders, pens, diskettes.
5. Consent forms.

Week 2: Writing on a Computer

1. Introduction of Story Book Weaver software to group.
2. Entering a program, opening a file, using the menu, using keyboard basics and mouse (handout, see Overview of Weekly Plans, Winter–Spring 1999), exiting a program, shutting down.
3. One facilitator works with small groups.
4. Computer activity: Creating a short text about family.
5. Print out texts and write comments in journal.
6. Group closure, comments, and feedback.

Week 3: School-Related Theme Presentation: *Leyendas* (Legends)

1. Explanation of KWLQ and use in journals.
2. Brainstorming session on legends.
3. Computer presentation: Introduction with large monitor to Internet (plus handout).
4. Opening Netscape, how to access a search engine, accessing Web sites, exiting the Internet.
5. Parents and children searching Internet and books for information on legends.
6. Group closure, comments, and feedback.

Week 4: Linking Project to School and the Writing Process

1. Discussion of project's importance and relation to school.
2. Field trip plans for visit to University of California, Santa Barbara.
3. Drafting a document on the computer.
4. Children begin writing about a legend with the help of parent or guardian.
5. Children report findings at close of session.
6. Group closure, comments, and feedback.

Week 5: Using Specific Software for Writing

1. Presentation to group on bilingual writing center with big-screen monitor.
2. Introduce parents and children to desktop publication of their work.
3. Computer presentation: How to change fonts, size, and style of text, adding accents and changing languages. How to print.
4. Brainstorm activity about legends.
5. Begin writing and printing out draft texts.
6. Group closure, comments, and feedback.

Week 6: The Design, Revision and Editing Processes Aided by Technology

1. Peer editing: Read each others' text and comment.
2. Organizing a text: Teacher-led story map activity.
3. Computer presentation: How to select, cut, and paste text.
4. Parents and children work together on texts at computer.
5. Group shares work: Reading aloud and/or providing comments on process.

Week 7: Continuing With Editing and Revision: Punctuation and Text Structure

1. Presentation to group on punctuation.
2. Computer activity: Using the spell check, checking the language, considering the options.
3. Work on a copy of first draft; that is, not the original text (to appreciate changes).
4. Print out text and share with group.
5. Group closure, comments, and feedback.

Week 8: Finalizing Editing and Computer Graphics

1. Parents and children finish editing texts on computer.
2. Group shares texts: Read aloud and feedback.
3. Computer activity: How to insert graphics and illustrate text.

4. Complete text and illustrations.
5. Print out final version to take home.
6. Group closure, comments, and feedback.

Week 9: Evaluating Progress and Internet Activity

1. Postquestionnaire and evaluation.
2. Computer activity: Parents and children work together through checklist at computer.
3. Final revisions to illustrations or texts.
4. Explore Internet: Check new sites and revisit familiar ones.
5. Reminders about last session and field trip.
6. Group closure, comments, and feedback.

Week 10: Last Session: Sharing the Publication

1. Completion of postquestionnaire and checklist.
2. Finish writing text about family (begun in Weeks 1 and 2).
3. Individual use of Internet.
4. Present anthology of legends to families.
5. Individuals read texts from desktop publication.
6. Group closure, comments, and feedback.
7. Social event.

Additional Activity: Parents and Children Field Trip to UCSB

1. Meet at school, 8:30 a.m.
2. Arrive at University tourist center: Reception and talk on higher education opportunities.
3. Tour of UCSB.
4. Lunch in the dorms.
5. Library presentation and visit.

Winter–Spring 1999

Week 1: Welcome and Overview

1. Introduction of project: Past members meet new members.
2. Prequestionnaire for newcomers.
3. Presentation of project theme: *Recuerdos* (Autobiographical memories).
4. Reading of Norma Cantú's work as an example.

5. Internet activity: Log on to site, research on personal/family name origins.
6. Group closure, comments, and feedback.

Week 2: Thinking About Writing and Technology

1. Elicitation of possible topics to write about: Brainstorming.
2. Ongoing parents: Begin drafting text on computer.
3. Newcomers: Introduction to bilingual writing center on computer.
4. Support for individuals from undergraduates.
5. Reminder about Club Proteo and special guest speaker next week.
6. Group closure, comments, and feedback.

Week 3: (New Recruitment) Links Between School and Home: Writing Ourselves

1. Introduction of visitors from UCSB and Mexico.
2. Presentation by Norma Cantú (1995) of *Life on the Frontera*: Alternative narrative.
3. Project participants read their texts to group.
4. Questions and discussions about literary and life experiences.
5. Internet activity: Cantú's Web page and information on Puebla, Mexico.
6. Group closure, comments, and feedback.

Week 4: Beginning a Document

1. Computer activity: Early arrivals use Internet or continue working on texts.
2. Group activity: Feedback and discussion from last session.
3. Reintroduce *Recuerdos* theme for all new members. Continuing members work on texts.
4. Presentation of bilingual writing center on large monitor for newcomers.
5. Print out drafts to take home and share with family and friends.
6. Group activity: Song and guitar playing from new member.

Week 5: Constructing a Narrative and Desktop Publishing

1. Reminder of theme for remaining sessions and the publication that will be produced with participants' contributions.
2. Children work with teacher, videotaping their narratives.
3. Adults and children work with assistance at the computers writing their texts.
4. Group activity: Share texts so far by reading aloud or simple talk about topic.
5. Songs from member on guitar accompanied by daughter.

6. Group closure, comments, and feedback.

Week 6: Developing a Sense of Narrative

1. Continue writing on narratives: Expanding details, thinking about audience.
2. Peer editing: Read and comment on partner's text.
3. Computer activity: Introduction of spell check feature for new members.
4. Encourage group to think about what they wish to express.
5. Group closure, comments, and feedback.

Week 7: Punctuation and Meaning Making

1. Refining the writing process.
2. Presentation on punctuation with a poem and examples.
3. Activity on punctuation: Identify and give example using material from poem in Spanish.
4. Close with a song.
5. Reminder to bring in photographs.
6. Group closure, comments, and feedback.

Week 8: Publishing and Literacy Practices in the Community

1. Special guests editors from *El Sol* newspaper.
2. Participants begin sorting work for publication.
3. Computer activity: Learning to scan photographs.
4. The editors of *El Sol* interview participants.
5. Ongoing Internet research: Interactive Web site on punctuation.
6. Group closure, comments, and feedback.

Week 9: Technology for Publishing

1. Continue scanning family photos and editing texts.
2. Insert scanned pictures into texts.
3. Literacy activities questionnaire.
4. Assist children with school project reports.
5. Internet free time.
6. Group closure, comments, and feedback.

Week 10: Thinking about Literacy Practices and Technology

1. Finalizing written texts and pictures.

2. Guest visitor from Mexico, UNAM.
3. Computer activity: Saving individual files to ZIP disk.
4. Follow-up interviews to literacy questionnaires.
5. Group closure, comments, and feedback.

Week 11: Finalize Narratives: Defining the Anthology

1. Work to complete texts.
2. Nominations and votes for publication's title.
3. Distribution of *El Sol* newspaper (article and interviews about project).
4. Postevaluation and independent Internet exploration.
5. Assistance to anyone who has still not finished their text.
6. Group closure, comments, and feedback.

Week 12: Literary Traditions and Cultural Links

1. Final session.
2. Guest speakers from Department of Spanish, UCSB.
3. The importance of Spanish literary tradition.
4. Distribution of final publication, *Recuerdos Profundos.*
5. Parents and children share their texts from the publication.
6. Group closure, comments, and feedback.
7. Social.

JOURNAL OF EDUCATION FOR STUDENTS PLACED AT RISK, 6(1&2), 115–132
Copyright © 2001, Lawrence Erlbaum Associates, Inc.

Bridging Funds of Distributed Knowledge: Creating Zones of Practices in Mathematics

Norma González

Bureau of Applied Research in Anthropology
University of Arizona

Rosi Andrade

Southwest Institute for Research on Women, Women's Studies
University of Arizona

Marta Civil

Department of Mathematics
University of Arizona

Luis Moll

Department of Language, Reading and Culture
University of Arizona

The work in this article has a basis in a long-term research paradigm investigating the "funds of knowledge" of diverse populations. This conceptualization adopts an anthropological perspective for viewing the households of low-income and minority students as repositories of diverse knowledge bases. In the BRIDGE project, the focus has been on understanding the mathematical potential of households, as well as "mathematizing" household practices. The transformation of mathematical knowledge, however, has been somewhat problematic. Our experience until now indicates that, whereas other classroom knowledge domains (language arts, social studies, etc.) may draw in a rather straightforward fashion from households, mathematical knowledge may not be so easily incorporated. This article describes a theoretical refinement

Requests for reprints should be sent to Norma González, P.O. Box 210030, University of Arizona, Tucson, AZ 85721–0030. E-mail: neg@u.arizona.edu

of the concept of funds of knowledge, and will endeavor to conceptualize the distributed nature of mathematical community capital.

As academic attention came to be directed on educational disparities of minority children in years past, there emerged a discourse that centered on educators coming to know the culture of their students. Predicated on the assumption that classroom cultural and linguistic patterns should be congruent with cultural and linguistic community patterns, researchers and practitioners sought to bridge what came to be regarded as the discontinuity or mismatch gap. Yet, in this postmodern and poststructuralist moment, traditional notions of culture have taken a theoretical beating (González, 1999). The essentialization and reification of bounded and shared cultural traits has not been adequate to conceptualize the translocal, transnational, and transborder communities that are the hallmark of globalization. The contested and contesting nature of culture no longer serves us well as we speak of diverse populations.

For several years, we have worked within a conceptual framework that has come to be known as the *funds of knowledge* perspective. This work has undergone several iterations (see González, 1995; González & Amanti, 1997; González et al., 1995; Moll, 1992; Moll, Amanti, Neff, & González, 1992; Moll & González, 1996). Initially drawing from the anthropological work of Wolf (1966), the term *funds of knowledge* was coined by Greenberg, an applied anthropologist at the University of Arizona (Vélez-Ibáñez & Greenberg, 1992). In the household funds paradigm, Wolf distinguished a number of funds households must juggle to make ends meet: caloric funds, funds of rent, replacement funds, ceremonial funds, social funds, and so on. Entailed in each is a wider set of activities requiring specific bodies, or funds, of knowledge. Funds of knowledge, then, are the historically accumulated bodies of knowledge and skills essential for household functioning and well-being.

The basic premise has been that classroom learning can be greatly enhanced when teachers learn more about their students and about their students' households. In our particular version of how this can be accomplished, we use ethnographic research methods involving participant observation, interviewing, and elicitation of narratives and reflection on field notes to flesh out the multidimensionality of student experience. Teachers venture into their students' households and communities, not as teachers attempting to convey educational information, but as learners seeking to understand the ways people make sense of their everyday lives.

Although the concept of making home visits is not new, entering the households of Mexican American, African American, and Native American students with an eye toward learning from them is a radical departure from traditional home visits. Drawing from ethnographic and qualitative techniques, teacher-researchers tap into the reservoirs of accumulated knowledge and strategies for survival that households possess. They are not given secondhand generalities about Latino, African American, or Native American culture by academic researchers; they are learning, as ethnographers, directly from interviews and other firsthand experiences. In contrast to other home visits, these visits are part of a "systematic, intentional inquiry by teachers" as Lytle and Cochran-Smith (1990, p. 84) defined teacher research, about their students' household life.

Our project has encompassed three interlocking areas (see Moll et al., 1992):

1. Community. This area has emphasized the local historical dimensions of households within regional sociopolitical and economic contexts. This broader view of the political ecology of households helps to reconceptualize them not as the source of barriers to educational attainment, but as repositories of resources that can be strategically tapped. Teacher-researchers interview household members regarding regional processes in household origins and development and the labor history of the families, which reveals some of the households' accumulated funds of knowledge (see Vélez-Ibáñez & Greenberg, 1992). In so doing, teacher-researchers have found that household knowledge is broad and diverse, and may include information about, for example, ranching, farming, and animal husbandry, which are associated with households' rural origins; or knowledge about construction and building, which are related to urban occupations; as well as knowledge about many other matters, such as trade, business, and finance on both sides of the border.

We have also been particularly interested in how families develop social networks that interconnect them with their environments (and most important with other households), and how these social relationships facilitate the development and exchange of resources, including funds of knowledge. A key characteristic of these exchanges is their reciprocity. These reciprocal social networks provide contexts in which learning can occur—contexts, for example, where children have ample opportunities to participate in activities with people they trust (Moll et al., 1992).

2. After-school lab/study groups. These are settings to share and reflect on household findings, and plan, develop, and support innovations in instruction. Within these study group meetings, ethnography surfaced as more than a series of techniques. It became the filter through which the households were conceptualized as multidimensional and vibrant entities. Although specific techniques in participant observation, field note writing, interviewing, and elicitation of life histories were presented, the focus was continuously on the constitutive and discursive properties of the joint construction of knowledge. It is in these meetings that we came to problematize and refine how this methodology can be applicable to the area of mathematics.

3. Classroom practice. This third arena has involved the incorporation of household knowledge bases into tangible curricular activities within the classroom. It is within this arena that teacher-researchers have mediated between home and school knowledge and links to student experience materialized in content areas.

BEYOND CULTURE

The careful integration of the three main components of our project—ethnographic community analysis, reflexive teacher study groups, and classroom application—has resulted in a successful blend for our local specificity. The methodology did not assume that teacher-researchers were looking for cultural traits to describe a population, which could then be imported into the classroom. Instead, teacher-researchers developed their own theories of households, of process, of social and culture theory, and were able to go beyond a mismatch paradigm. By building on students' strengths, in whatever area, teachers could lay a foundation for higher order content-based learning. Entering households with a funds of knowledge perspective engendered two transformative shifts in how households are conceptualized. The first concerns a revision in the definition of culture of the households, and the second concerns an alternative to the deficit model of households.

Viewing households within a processual view of culture, that is, one that is rooted in the lived contexts of their students, highlights a conceptualization of culture as negotiated over contested domains, and not, for example, a static grab bag of food, dances, and celebrations. Our emphasis was on practice as theorized by Bourdieu (1977), Williams (1977), and the writings of Foucault (1970, 1972, 1980), and we emphasized what it is that people actually do and what they say about what they do. Teacher-researchers were thus able to locate and reflect on the lived practices of their students.

The second shift centered on household analysis carried out by teacher-researchers, which constructs households not as barren of social and cognitive resources for children's learning, but as landscapes that can be scratched to reveal underlying resources that might not be readily apparent. As teachers validated household praxis as being imbued with resources worthy of pedagogical notice, parents came to authenticate their own skills as meaningful and productive.

BUILDING BRIDGES TO MATHEMATICAL FUNDS OF KNOWLEDGE

The differences and apparent lack of connection between in-school and outside-school mathematics have been well documented in a number of studies (Abreu, 1995; Bishop & Abreu, 1991; Carraher, Carraher, & Schliemann, 1985; Lave, 1988; Saxe, 1991; Schoenfeld, 1991) that indicate that both adults and students are competent in performing mathematical tasks that they view as relevant. The practically error-free arithmetic in everyday situations provides a dramatic contrast with low performance in school-like circumstances. Although we had affirmed that a funds of knowledge perspective could impact content areas such as language arts and social studies (Amanti, 1995; Floyd-Tenery, 1995; Hensley,

1995; Moll, 1992), the areas of mathematics and science were more problematic. It was to this end that the BRIDGE project was conceptualized. Could a funds of knowledge methodology, through ethnographic understanding of a community, reveal mathematical funds of knowledge that could impact classroom practice?

First of all, we had to understand the nature of classroom practice in mathematics. What is behind the leap to irrelevance once mathematics is moved into the classroom? The recent calls for changes in mathematics education (National Council of Teachers of Mathematics, Commission on Standards for School Mathematics, 1989; National Research Council, 1989) capitalize on the need to teach mathematics to all children, to help them make connections with their everyday world, to engage them in doing mathematics and in constructing meanings, and to move away from the teacher and textbook as the authority on what counts as mathematical activity.

However, because the discourse in mathematics has presented a Eurocentric and androcentric perspective on the development of knowledge and civilization, the domain of mathematics has been embedded in these frames of reference. Frankenstein and Powell (1994) presented cogent evidence of the "distorted and hidden history of mathematical knowledge" (p. 88), which has obscured the contributions to mathematical knowledge of those outside the rational, Western, male elite discourse (see McBride, 1989). Mathematical knowledge has resonated with unequal power relations. The images, texts, and discourse of mathematicians have not included perspectives on the situated nature of knowledge, nor on the language of power that often drives the pursuit of knowledge.

What does this mean in reference to diverse students learning mathematics? The impact of these discourses is poignantly stated by Rich, writing on "Invisibility in Academe": "When someone with the authority of a teacher, say, describes the world and you are not in it, there is a moment of psychic disequilibrium, as if you looked into a mirror and saw nothing" (quoted in Rosaldo, 1989, p. ix). At a macro, taken-as-shared, mathematical level, these students do not exist as mathematicians. As Fasheh (1991) noted in his personal narrative outlining the role that mathematics plays in constructing symbolic power, "Hegemony is not only characterized by what it includes, but also by what it excludes; by what it renders marginal, deems inferior and makes invisible" (p. 59). Minority and linguistically diverse students in general have not been constructed as visible players within mathematical discourses either in or out of schools.

One of the aims of the BRIDGE project, then, was to ask the following questions: What counts as mathematics? How can we find mathematics within households that are economically marginal? How can we help parents and communities see themselves as mathematicians, "doing" mathematics in their everyday lives? Our avenue to accomplishing these aims was to adopt our previous methodology, but to focus only on mathematics. The household interviews were revised to highlight labor histories that could be rich in mathematical potential.

WHAT DID WE FIND?

We began with the assumption that uncovering mathematical funds of knowledge would not be very different from discovering knowledge bases in other domains, such as literacy or language use. Because households regularly utilize mathematical resources in some form, we felt these would be easily observable and accessible. Initially, it seemed that this was the case. As teacher-researchers entered the households armed with a lens to focus on mathematics within households, the mathematics of cooking, construction, and sewing, as well as the logical processes of schedule setting and time management were all evident. After this initial affirmation of mathematical processes, though, our study group was faced with a discomfiting reality. Although teacher-researchers found the aforementioned reservoirs of knowledge in households, the underlying mathematical principles were not always evident to household members. For instance, construction workers could explain their methods for tile setting and framing a house, but on deeper questioning, they could not elucidate why these methods worked. Similarly, seamstresses could produce wonderfully complex designs and patterns, but often the creation of these designs and patterns was a matter of trial and error rather than a logical progression. More disconcerting was the dawning realization that our mathematics researchers found it difficult to find the mathematics in many of these activities. Marta Civil, the mathematics educator in our group, often felt that her lack of knowledge with the practice itself (e.g., sewing) made it harder to "visualize" the mathematics, and that her training in academic and school math made it harder to see other forms of mathematics.

We want to emphasize that we were convinced that the split between school contexts of mathematics and community contexts of mathematics was not due to the socioeconomic status of the households. Instead, it seemed to be a matter of perspective. On the one hand, although the households we interviewed certainly deployed mathematical concepts, the academic transformation of those concepts was elusive. On the other hand, academically validated school knowledge of math seemed to obscure nonacademic forms of mathematical practices.

This left us in a theoretical vacuum. We were in need of further theorizing on how funds of knowledge could be applicable within the domain of mathematics. We had found that a linear transference of mathematical knowledge from household to classroom was problematic. Yet, we were aware that deep and rich mathematical processes were being tapped in the forms of constructions, buildings, landscapes, gardens, and clothing. To account for this distributed knowledge, we activated our own funds of knowledge and drew from the insights of Vygotsky and his theory of socially mediated knowledge.

The Significance of Vygotsky

The essence of Vygotsky was significant for our dilemma: Human thinking develops through the mediation of others (see Moll, in press). Put succinctly, people interact with their worlds, which are humanized through mediational means and practices. This mediation of actions through artifacts and practices, especially the uses of languages in both their oral and written forms, plays a crucial role in the formation and development of human intellectual capacities.

Vygotsky (1978, 1987) concentrated primarily on what he called *psychological tools,* the semiotic potential of systems of signs and symbols, most significantly language, in mediating thinking and the making of meaning (see also Wertsch, 1985, 1991). Nevertheless, however crucial these psychological tools may be to the mediation and development of thinking, the construction of meaning is regulated (or mediated) by social relationships (see Lee & Smagorinsky, 2000). It is in connection to this social emphasis that Vygotsky proposed the well-known concept of the zone of proximal development (ZPD), the contrast between what a child can do independently, representing his or her actual level of development, and what a child can do with the assistance of others, representing the proximal level of development (Vygotsky, 1978). Much has been written about this concept in recent years (cf. Moll, 1990; Wells, 1999), and we do not intend to spill any more ink on the subject. However, for our purposes here, we do want to emphasize the importance of a broader understanding of the ZPD, understood not only in terms of more capable others assisting less capable ones, but in terms of how human beings "use social processes and cultural resources of all kinds" (Scribner, 1990, p. 92) in helping children construct their futures.

In this broader sense, the concept of the ZPD was also used by Vygotsky to capture the relationship in schooling between what he called everyday and scientific concepts (Vygotsky, 1987, 1934/1994). The key difference between the two is that scientific or schooled concepts (e.g., mammals and socialism), as compared to everyday concepts (e.g., boats and cars), are systematic; that is, they form part of and are acquired though a system of formal instruction. It is not so much that one is acquired in school and the other out of school. Instead, Vygotsky emphasized the systematicity of how scientific concepts form part of an organized system of knowledge and can thus be more easily reflected on and manipulated deliberately; consequently, through schooling, these concepts become objects of study. Furthermore, Vygotsky (1987) pointed out the reciprocal relation between everyday and scientific concepts and how they mediate each other. Everyday concepts provide the conceptual fabric for the development of schooled concepts, but are also transformed through their connection to the more systematic concepts; scientific concepts grow into the everyday, into the domain of personal experience, acquiring meaning and significance. Yet these inscribe a conscious awareness and control onto the everyday, which he believed to be essential characteristics of schooling. This latter insight was crucial to us as we contemplated the in-school and outside-school contexts of mathematics.

How could we relate Vygotsky's theories to the practices we were encountering in our research on mathematics in households? One of the most provocative ideas to come out of Vygotskian-based psychology is that of distributed cognition (Salomon, 1993), and this was our theoretical starting block. Stated briefly, thinking is usually considered to take place solely within the head of the individual, what some psychologists refer to as "solo" or "in-the-head" cognition. Schools accept this notion, testing students to determine their individual ability or intelligence, considered as an immutable, fixed attribute or trait. Conclusions about children's abilities (as measured by the tests) are reached readily by many educators. These conclusions are usually connected to the children's social class background, if we are to judge by the sort of rigid and prescribed schooling lower social class groups receive. In contrast, conceptions of human activity, including intellectual activity, as mediated and distributed bring about a radically different idea about thinking (Moll, in press). The key point is that human beings and their social worlds are inseparable. They are embedded in each other; thus, human thinking is irreducible to individual properties or traits. Instead, it is always mediated, distributed among persons, artifacts, activities, and settings (cf. Pea, 1993). People think in conjunction with the artifacts and resources of their social worlds and these artifacts and resources, in turn, are found in their social worlds, and made available through the social relationships and settings within which human beings constitute their lives. Schools and households are two such settings. However, as Cole and Engestrom (1993) observed, "Precisely how cognition is distributed must be worked out for different kinds of activity, with their different forms of mediation, division of labor, social rules and so on" (p. 42). How social relationships, ideas, or activities become resources for thinking, then, must be studied in relation to the concrete and varied practices of human beings. It was this idea that led to our rethinking of how we had been investigating the mathematical practices in households. In the next section, we describe how participation in a zone of practice integrated social relationships and activities into a finished product.

THE MATHEMATICAL PRACTICE OF A FEMALE TAILOR DESIGNING AND MAKING A DRESS PATTERN

As the BRIDGE project progressed, we realized that although we had rich information based on household interviews of mathematical activities, we did not have a sense of actual participation in these activities. In eliciting information from the households, we had not adopted a stance of coparticipants in mathematical practices. We had been more observers than participants. It was evident that putting the participant back into participant observation was necessary. At this point, within the study group format, we decided to build on work that had been emerging from another arena.

A teacher-researcher, Hilda González, who had participated in the original work that had been undertaken on literacy practices in the home, had continued her work in this area while pursuing a doctoral degree. Her interest was in not only documenting the funds of knowledge in literacy that are found in households, but in doing so in a way that was more participatory and reciprocal (González-Angiulo, 1998).

To this end, she formed a mothers' literature circle as a way of creating intertextual experiences between the mothers' lives and the themes of widely read books. By bringing these themes to a discursive consciousness, the women made connections to issues of social criticism in their own lives and came to a historical consciousness of how they came to be where they are now.

Conceptualized as a critique of the passive documentation of household funds of knowledge, the Señoras' literature circle was made up of mothers of children who attended a school within an "at-risk" area. The mothers, mostly immigrant women, met and, as of this writing, continue to meet once a week. The literature circle encompassed the domains of multiple literacies, and the mothers began to see themselves as producers as well as consumers of knowledge. Andrade, Moll, and González Le Denmat (in press) explained the process of connecting the participants' experience in the world to their reading of texts:

> It is too varied, dynamic, even unpredictable, and it includes a range of modes of engagement which test, from preoccupations of decoding smoothly to extracting insights about the role of language and social relationships in life. And the book [or activity] becomes, throughout the women's actions with it, another social environment or context within which to develop new knowledge and experiences, new social identities, if you will.

It was a small leap then, to introduce mathematics into this forum. What was true of the literature study group became true of the mathematics study group: The discussions that took place were but a vehicle for the transformations that occur as a result of the sharing and cocreation of knowledge and experience. What each participant brings to this experience and consequently takes away is multiplex. The study group was a safe place where one could question, discuss, comment, critique, and analyze in a mutually educative process.

The Activity

On this early morning, Señora María, as she is respectfully addressed, offered to give a lesson on sewing in a format similar to our study group. Señora María is an immigrant woman in her 50s who works from her home, caring for her family, nieces, nephews, and grandchildren while practicing her profession as tailor. More than 20 women are participating in the group, including three of us.

Señora María began by walking us through the taking of measurements and design of a three-part pattern for a dress (front and back of the upper part, and the skirt). Teacher Hilda González was volunteered as the model for the group. Throughout the several hours that elapsed during the course of this lesson, the other women in the group shared their knowledge of sewing, exchanging tricks of the trade and asking one another how to do certain things (e.g., how to make shorts or a flounced skirt; how to make a rounded collar stay flat).

After the key measurements (back, bust, length of upper body, waist, hips, and length of upper skirt) had been taken, Señora María drew a rectangle, which eventually would become both the front and the back half of the upper portion of the dress. The concept of symmetry would be used in making the other half. The tools of Señora María's trade used in the day's lesson included a square ruler and a measuring tape. With these, Señora María demonstrated flexibility with mathematical knowledge rooted in past formal educational experiences, as she had learned her profession at a trade school in Mexico.

Marta Civil, the mathematics educator in our group, admitted that seeing Señora María develop this drawing and listening to her say things such as, "Waist is 70 cm, let's add 6 because we need 3 for each pleat, and then we divide by 4," was as "mesmerizing and mysterious to her as mathematics lectures are to so many people seeing bits and pieces but not getting the whole picture." Yet, it did not seem as mysterious to the other women in the group because they were much more familiar with the practice. Further, the collective knowledge and experience of the group on the topic of sewing and the manufacture of clothing (as learned through the scrutiny practiced in purchasing various types and styles of clothing) allowed a dialogue of sophisticated meanings to be constructed. Throughout the lesson, the repeated "ahs" from the group demonstrated that Señora María's explanations facilitated understanding. However, for Civil, the mathematics educator, the lack of familiarity with making patterns for sewing and her formal training in mathematics seemed to be clear obstacles to her understanding of the conversation. This episode reminded Civil of Fasheh's (1991) account of his relationship to mathematics versus his mother's relationship to mathematics in her sewing:

> It struck me that the math she was using was beyond my comprehension; moreover, while math for me was the subject matter I studied and taught, for her it was basic to the operation of her understanding. ... Without the official ideological support system, no one would have "needed" my math; ... in contrast, my mother's math was so deeply embedded in the culture that it was invisible through eyes trained by formal education. ... Mathematics was integrated into her world as it never was into mine. (p. 58)

This was a crucial insight: The validation and privileging of academic mathematics was completely dependent on an "ideological support system" that constructed the hegemony of a particular type of mathematics. On the other hand, the mathematics of Fasheh's (1991) mother "was so deeply embedded ... that it was invisible through eyes trained by formal education" (p. 58). This kind of mathematics goes beyond facile constructs of social context and must take into account the deeply felt relationships of coparticipants, the social relationships involved in undertaking the practices, and the deep engagement of connection with a product, not just a process.

Señora María and the women in the group were interested in making a skirt. Their object was not to uncover mathematics in this process. Yet the participation of Civil transformed the social interaction into one in which the concepts could be systematized instead of intuited. The shift in contexts problematized the notion of who held the spontaneous everyday concepts and who held the scientific or schooled concepts. The systematicity of the mothers' knowledge was based on familiarity with the practices involved. As Civil questioned the how and the why of the calculations, the answers seemed to be obvious to the mothers; yet, Civil admitted, they were difficult for her to visualize.

Additionally, the actual practices required skills and knowledge in other areas: efficient cutting, conservation of resources by using less paper for the actual pattern, and problem solving. In one example, the construction of a quarter of a circle, we can see the systematicity of everyday mathematics based on practice. To make the pattern for the skirt, Señora María took a large square of paper and, holding her measuring tape fixed at one corner of her square (the center), she marked a few points 25 cm from that center point. She then joined them to get a quarter of a circle (Figure 1).

Why 25 cm for the radius? She came up with 25 by taking one third of the waist measurement (to which she previously had added a few extra centimeters for the pleats). Then, based on the person's height and the favored length of the skirt, she drew another quarter of a circle, using the same technique. Figure 2 demonstrates the next step.

She cut out the smaller quarter of a circle, which was to become then one half of the skirt (Figure 3).

Constructing the circles (or quarter of a circle) as she did certainly shows the circle as the geometric locus of points equidistant from a given point. This is the formal definition of a circle. Yet we wonder how many children experience this in school mathematics (instead of simply using a compass to draw a circle). Even more, we wonder how many children are aware that this knowledge about circles

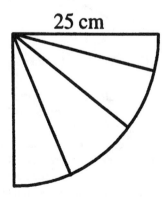

25 cm

FIGURE 1   Drawing a quarter of a circle.

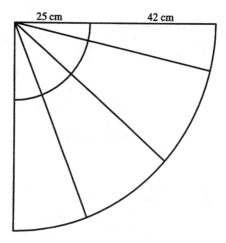

FIGURE 2   Toward a skirt 42 cm long.

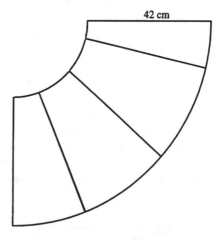

FIGURE 3   Half of the skirt.

may reside in their households. Would using a compass be considered more mathematical than using the tape measure (or a ruler) to mark a few points equidistant from a given point and then joining them? This concept of what we count as being mathematics is related to our values and beliefs about what mathematics is. In particular, in this context, we are reminded of the work of Harris (1987), in which she compared the mathematics behind the design of the heel of a sock, something that a woman is likely to do, versus the mathematics behind the design of a right-angle cylindrical pipe. Although the latter is considered a mathematical problem, the former is not.

In this example, we found that mathematics is not a possession residing within the head of participants. It was not an immutable, fixed attribute or trait of one individual. Rather, mathematics was a practice, but we had to discover how to create a zone for the development of that practice. It is not enough to simply "possess" funds of knowledge in mathematical domains. These must be socially mediated into productive knowledge to be meaningful. We reiterate: The key point is that human beings and their social worlds are inseparable—they are embedded in each other; thus, human thinking is irreducible to individual properties or traits. Instead, it is always mediated, distributed among persons, artifacts, activities, and settings.

Within this example we find evidence of mathematics embedded in social knowledge. However, it must be mediated through the activity of the group, the artifact of the sewing patterns and tools, and distributed among the participants of the group, including those with more formal academic knowledge. This was the key that unlocked our previous disjunction in finding mathematical funds of knowledge in households. We had attempted to disembed this knowledge from its social meaning and access it through a linear process of dialogue. We did not consider the shared and collective construction of mathematical knowledge that is often outside of the purview of individual households.

We began with a theoretical posture that underscored the uneven distribution of knowledge; that is to say, culture could not account for the everyday lived experiences of every household. Our emphasis on practices of households, on what they actually do, helped us to conceptualize mathematics in households. However, our method for doing this, through the narrative elicitation of overt and covert mathematical processes, decontextualized mathematics from its embeddedness in social activities. We had attempted to decouple doing mathematics from its ZPD; that is, from interaction with others. When we viewed a community knowledge base within an authentic setting, with a group of mothers intent on accomplishing a specific goal, the socially mediated nature of mathematical meaning making came into focus.

CONCLUSIONS

In our theoretical refinement of a funds of knowledge methodology, we have come to acknowledge that we must go beyond a simplistic dichotomy between community (practical, outside-school, intuitive, tacit), and academic (in-school, deliberate, explicit) mathematics. Our experience with the mothers' group demonstrates that the forms of meaning making in which the mothers engaged can be characterized by the principles that undergird effective classroom instruction: authentic engagement in joint productive activity, connecting to prior knowledge, complexity and rigor, and the dialogical emergence of instruction.

Returning again to Vygotsky and his insights on everyday and scientific understanding, we reiterate that the difference between the two is not that one is acquired in school and the other out of school. Instead, what is at issue is systematicity. Scientific (or mathematical) concepts form part of an organized system of knowledge. However, we also have demonstrated the systematicity of Señora María's informal practices. As Vygotsky postulated, we found a reciprocal relation between everyday and scientific concepts. Although everyday concepts provide the building blocks for the development of schooled concepts, they can be transformed through a connection with the academic. Similarly, scientific concepts can be transformed into the everyday, into the domain of practice, acquiring meaning and significance, but also enabling conscious reflection and meta-awareness.

Community funds of mathematical knowledge reside in distributed everyday and scientific knowledge that does not have to be reconstituted anew at every turn. Accessing this knowledge, however, is not an individual construction, but is socially mediated through more knowledgeable others. However, we must remain aware of the dialectical relationship between the academic and the everyday, and of the fact that the category of more knowledgeable others is a shifting construct.

What does this mean for educational practice? It means that we can create zones of practice, and we can invite children into a world with a concrete motivating activity in which the everyday and spontaneous come into contact with the scientific and the schooled. The dichotomy of in-school and outside-school mathematics can be elided into a dialectical practice within which students' engagement with both the activity and the social context are foregrounded. The mothers' study group created a practice zone for Civil, but Civil also created a mathematical zone for the mothers, and we came to an appreciation of how contexts are constituted by the contributions of the participants. Does this imply a mathematically sophisticated teacher? Yes, in some ways. However, although it might be more difficult to create these zones of mathematical practice, it is very much worthwhile. Many teachers create such zones in domains such as literacy and language arts, but a "whole mathematics" classroom similar to a whole-language classroom often remains uncharted terrain.

What suggestions can we offer? First, we have to return to the initial assumptions of our approach, and underscore that practices may not be uniformly distributed throughout a community. Thus a community of practice might encompass contested and contesting ways of sense making. It is therefore important to look at the local contexts of practices and to acknowledge that uniform patterns might not be consensually agreed on or taken for granted. Indeed, subaltern discourses may construct particular forms of practice.

Second, we must be aware of the social relationships of participants in any given activity. This is evident as we think about more capable others, as there are social issues of relative status surrounding the construction of knowledge. When we have carried out observations in classrooms, it is often the case that students are keenly aware of classroom social status, and negotiation of mathematical discourse is often less a function of coconstruction than it is one of jockeying for position within the social hierarchy. Students often accept as "givens" the answers supplied by the more popular students or the gifted and talented education (GATE) students, and regularly disregard the answers contributed by those outside of the social loop. The existence of special programs for "special" children (whether "gifted" or "slow") puts students in cubby holes and creates a set of expectations that influences the learning dynamics. Placement in GATE makes these students intelligent to the rest of their peers. This clearly affects the creation of an environment conducive to a mathematical discussion, as these children's statements are clearly more valued and legitimated by their classmates. In contrast, in the mothers' group, the women were equally validated as producers of legitimated knowledge by each other.

A third point concerns the kind of mathematics that mathematics educators assume students should be doing, especially as is relates to the perceived dichotomy between schooled and everyday mathematics. For example, Civil, with a formal academic background in mathematics, experiences mathematical explorations as a form of playfulness and finds enjoyment in discovering patterns in seemingly very different situations. We suspect that many of the math educators who are working on developing "classroom cultures in which students *do* mathematics naturally" (Schoenfeld, 1987, pp. 214–215), share a similar orientation toward mathematics.

Constructivist approaches support a perception of mathematics as a creative art form, as a form of playfulness. Yet, these are constructs of adult mathematicians, not of novice users. Instruction in mathematics continues to be defined in many cases as the development of novel methods to express and transmit mathematical representations that are self-evident to the expert. However, as Lemke (1990) cogently argued,

> The knowledge of mathematics consists of two parts: a practical knowledge of how to perform various manipulations of quantitative and logical relationships, and a theoretical knowledge of how those relationships fit together to form an overall system within which the manipulations make sense. It is only the first part that most people have any conceivable use for, but it is only the second part that enables you to understand why mathematical procedures work. ... For nearly all students, abstract theoretical mathematics will remain a luxury, not a necessity, in their educations. While it should certainly be available to those students who want to study it, perhaps we should be honest with all students about the role of mathematics as a "tool" subject and the real reasons why they don't understand how it works. (pp. 164–165)

By not being honest with students about the adult mathematical experts' agenda in mathematics education, students do not view the playfulness of the second part of mathematics to which Lemke (1990) referred as a legitimate use of mathematics. Mathematics becomes subsumed under a veneer of positivistic assumptions that label knowledge as correct apprehensions of taken-as-shared mathematical principles, not open to challenge. We suggest that reform efforts in mathematics pay closer attention to the social worlds of children (cf. Andrade & Moll, 1993) in all of their multidimensionality to better formulate a child's-eye view of the forms and functions of mathematical discourses.

Finally, and perhaps most important, we learned from our experience that mathematics practices cannot be disembedded from social context, and that creating a zone of mathematical practice depends on not only the store of funds of knowledge, but the transformation of that knowledge into meaningful activity. Like the mothers in the study group, students must be involved in practices in which they are not only consumers of knowledge, but producers of mathematical practices.

ACKNOWLEDGMENTS

This work was supported under the Education Research and Development Program (PR/Award R306A60001), the Center for Research on Education, Diversity and Excellence, as administered by the Office of Educational Research and Improvement (OERI), National Institute on the Education of At-Risk Students (NIEARS), and the U.S. Department of Education (USDOE).

The contents, findings, and opinions expressed in this article are those of the authors and do not necessarily represent the positions or policies of OERI, NIEARS, or the USDOE.

We also would like to thank Roland Tharp for conversations that helped lead to insights in this article.

REFERENCES

Abreu, G. de. (1995). Understanding how children experience the relationship between home and school mathematics. *Mind, Culture, and Activity, 2,* 119–142.

Amanti, C. (1995). Teachers doing research: Beyond classroom walls. *Practicing Anthropology, 17*(3), 7–9.

Andrade, R. A. C., & Moll, L. (1993). The social worlds of children: An emic view. *Journal of the Society for Accelerative Learning and Teaching, 18*(1–2), 81–125.

Andrade, R., Moll, L. C., & González Le Denmat, H. (in press). El grupo de las señoras: Creating consciousness through literature. In S. Hollingsworth & M. Gallego (Eds.), *Challenging a single standard: Multiple perspectives on literacy.* New York: Teachers College Press.

Bishop, A., & Abreu, G. de. (1991). Children's use of outside-school knowledge to solve mathematics problems in-school. In F. Furinghetti (Ed.), *Proceedings of the fifteenth International Conference for the Psychology of Mathematics Education, 1,* 128–135.

Bourdieu, P. (1977). *Outline of a theory of practice.* Cambridge, England: Cambridge University Press.

Carraher, T., Carraher, D., & Schliemann, A. (1985). Mathematics in the streets and in the schools. *British Journal of Developmental Psychology, 3,* 21–29.

Cole, M., & Engestrom, Y. (1993). A cultural-historical approach to distributed cognition. In G. Salomon (Ed.), *Distributed cognition* (pp. 1–46). Cambridge, England: Cambridge University Press.

Fasheh, M. (1991). Mathematics in a social context: Math within education as praxis versus math within education as hegemony. In M. Harris (Ed.), *Schools, mathematics and work* (pp. 57–61). New York: Falmer.

Floyd-Tenery, M. (1995). Teacher as mediator. *Practicing Anthropology, 17*(3), 10–12.

Foucault, M. (1970). *The order of things: An archaeology of the human sciences.* New York: Pantheon.

Foucault, M. (1972). *The archaeology of knowledge and the discourse on language.* New York: Pantheon.

Foucault, M. (1980). *Power/knowledge: Selected interviews and other writings 1972–1977.* Brighton, England: Harvester.

Frankenstein, M., & Powell, A. (1994). Toward liberatory mathematics: Paulo Freire's epistemology and ethnomathematics. In P. L. McLaren & C. Lankshear (Eds.), *Politics of liberation: Paths from Freire* (pp. 74–99). New York: Routledge.

González, N. (1995). Processual approaches to multicultural education. *Journal of Applied Behavioral Science, 31,* 234–244.

González, N. (1999). What will we do when culture does not exist anymore? *Anthropology and Education Quarterly, 30,* 431–435.

González, N., & Amanti, C. (1997). Teaching anthropological methods to teachers: The transformation of knowledge. In C. Kottak, J. White, R. Furlow, & P. Rice (Eds.), *The teaching of anthropology: Problems, issues and decisions* (pp. 353–359). Mountain View, CA: Mayfield.

González, N., Moll, L., Floyd-Tenery, M., Rivera A., Rendon, P., Gonzales, R., & Amanti, C. (1995). Funds of knowledge for teaching in Latino households. *Urban Education, 29,* 444–471.

González-Angiulo, H. (1998). *Señoras: From funds of knowledge to self discovery.* Unpublished doctoral dissertation, University of Arizona, Tucson, AZ.

Harris, M. (1987). An example of traditional women's work as a mathematics resource. *For the Learning of Mathematics, 7*(3), 26–28.

Hensley, M. (1995). From untapped potential to creative realization: Empowering parents. *Practicing Anthropology, 17*(3), 13–16.

Lave, J. (1988). *Cognition in practice: Mind mathematics and culture in everyday life.* New York: Cambridge University Press.

Lee, C. D., & Smagorinsky, P. (Eds.). (2000). *Vygotskian perspectives on literacy research: Constructing meaning through collaborative activity.* Cambridge, England: Cambridge University Press.

Lemke, J. L. (1990). *Talking science: Language, learning and values.* Norwood, NJ: Ablex.

Lytle, S., & Cochran-Smith, M. (1990). Learning from teacher research: A working typology. *Teachers College Record, 92,* 83–103.

McBride, M. (1989). A Foucauldian analysis of mathematical discourse. *For the Learning of Mathematics, 9*(1), 40–46.

Moll, L. C. (Ed.). (1990). *Vygotsky and education.* Cambridge, England: Cambridge University Press.

Moll, L. C. (1992). Bilingual classrooms and community analysis: Some recent trends. *Educational Researcher, 21*(2), 20–24.

Moll, L. C. (in press). Through the mediation of others: Vygotskian research on teaching. In V. Richardson (Ed.), *Handbook of research on teaching* (4th ed.). Washington, DC: American Educational Research Association.

Moll, L., Amanti, C., Neff, D., & González, N. (1992). Funds of knowledge for teaching: A qualitative approach to developing strategic connections between homes and classrooms. *Theory Into Practice, 31,* 132–141.

Moll, L., & González, N. (1996). Teachers as social scientists: Learning about culture from household research. In P. M. Hall (Ed.), *Race, ethnicity and multiculturalism: Missouri Symposium on Research and Educational Policy* (Vol. 1, pp. 89–114). New York: Garland.

National Council of Teachers of Mathematics, Commission on Standards for School Mathematics. (1989). *Curriculum and evaluation standards for school mathematics.* Reston, VA: Author.

National Research Council. (1989). *Everybody counts: A report to the nation on the future of mathematics education.* Washington, DC: National Academy Press.

Pea, R. (1993). Practices of distributed intelligence and designs for education. In G. Salomon (Ed.), *Distributed cognition* (pp. 47–87). Cambridge, England: Cambridge University Press.

Rosaldo, R. (1989). *Culture and truth: The remaking of social analysis.* Boston: Beacon.

Salomon, G. (1993). *Distributed cognition.* Cambridge, England: Cambridge University Press.

Saxe, G. (1991). *Culture and cognitive development: Studies in mathematical understanding.* Hillsdale, NJ: Lawrence Erlbaum Associates, Inc.

Schoenfeld, A. (1987). What's all the fuss about metacognition? In A. H. Schoenfeld (Ed.), *Cognitive science and mathematics education* (pp. 189–215). Hillsdale, NJ: Lawrence Erlbaum Associates, Inc.

Schoenfeld, A. (1991). On mathematics as sense-making: An informal attack on the unfortunate divorce of formal and informal mathematics. In J. F. Voss, S. N. Perkins, & J. Segal (Eds.), *Informal reasoning and instruction* (pp. 311–343). Hillsdale, NJ: Lawrence Erlbaum Associates, Inc.

Scribner, S. (1990). Reflections on a model. *The Quarterly Newsletter of the Laboratory of Comparative Human Cognition, 12*(3), 90–94.

Vélez-Ibáñez, C., & Greenberg, J. (1992). Formation and transformation of funds of knowledge among U.S. Mexican households. *Anthropology and Education Quarterly, 23,* 313–335.

Vygotsky, L. S. (1978). *Mind in society.* Cambridge, MA: Harvard University Press.

Vygotsky, L. S. (1987). Problems of general psychology. In L. S. Vygotsky, *Collected works: Vol. 1* (R. Rieber & A. Carton, Eds.; N. Minick, Trans.). New York: Plenum.

Vygotsky, L. S. (1994). The development of academic concepts in school aged children. In R. Van der Veer & J. Valsiner (Eds.), *The Vygotsky reader* (pp. 355–370). Oxford, England: Blackwell. (Original work published 1934)

Wells, G. (1999). *Dialogic inquiry: Toward a sociocultural practice and theory of education.* Cambridge, England: Cambridge University Press.

Wertsch, J. (1985). *Vygotsky and the social formation of mind.* Cambridge, MA: Harvard University Press.

Wertsch, J. (1991). *Voices of the mind: A sociocultural approach to mediated action.* Cambridge, MA: Harvard University Press.

Williams, R. (1977). *Marxism and literature.* Oxford, England: Oxford University Press.

Wolf, E. (1966). *Peasants.* Englewood Cliffs, NJ: Prentice Hall.

JOURNAL OF EDUCATION FOR STUDENTS PLACED AT RISK, 6(1&2), 133–155
Copyright © 2001, Lawrence Erlbaum Associates, Inc.

Segregated Classrooms, Integrated Intent: How One School Responded to the Challenge of Developing Positive Interethnic Relations

Rosemary C. Henze

ARC Associates
Oakland, California

Children who feel unsafe in school because of threats of violence or verbal abuse based on race, ethnicity, or language cannot focus on the learning and achievement goals that the U.S. educational system has placed before us in the form of national standards. A primary need for some schools is to create a safe and secure environment and to ensure that children and adults of different backgrounds feel respected. Yet this raises an interesting question: Can schools be vehicles for improving race relations? In this article, I draw on a case study of 1 elementary school, Cornell,[1] to examine this question in depth. Many would answer that, given historical inequities such as segregation and tracking, schools are unlikely places for improvements in race or ethnic relations to take place. On the other hand, schools do create cultures and norms of their own that may deviate in some ways from the national culture, and in this sense they represent a potential site for change in race relations, at least locally.

During the past 3 years, several colleagues and I have carried out a research project called Leading for Diversity to document proactive approaches that school leaders are using to reduce racial and ethnic conflict and to promote positive interethnic relations (Henze, Katz, Norte, Sather, & Walker, 1999). One of the assumptions underlying this work is that schools can indeed make a positive difference in race relations, and therefore the activities they engage in to do so are worth documenting so that others can learn from them.

In the process of visiting many of the 21 schools participating in the study, I was from time to time challenged to look critically at this assumption. Can schools re-

---

Requests for reprints should be sent to Rosemary C. Henze, ARC Associates, 1212 Broadway, Suite 400, Oakland, CA 94612. E-mail: rhenze@arcassociates.org
[1]The school and individuals mentioned in this article have been assigned pseudonyms to protect the confidentiality of information shared.

ally be vehicles for improving race relations? On what basis can we answer this positively? What evidence is there to suggest that schools, as currently configured, cannot serve this function, or can only serve it partially? This article explores these questions in the context of one particular elementary school, Cornell, which served a diverse population of vibrant, hopeful children from low-income homes.

Kozol (1991) wrote that "Most of the urban schools I visited were 95 to 99 percent nonwhite" (p. 3) and "reminded me of garrisons or outposts in a foreign nation" (p. 5). He questioned why, in a country that calls itself a democracy, "we would agree to let our children go to school in places where no politician, school board president, or business CEO would dream of working" (p. 5). What emerges from his analysis, and from that of others such as McDermott and Varenne (1995), is the flip side of the traditional risk equation. These scholars, rather than focusing on factors in families and children that may predict school failure, asked instead how schools fail students and families, and indeed how our school system is structured so tightly around the label of "at riskness" that there is a necessary corollary: In addition to children acquiring at-risk factors, the at-risk label has to acquire children. We have, according to McDermott and Varenne, developed a culture that requires some of its members to be disabled, poor, illiterate, and low achieving.

Although many schools work hard, often against great odds, to address risk factors such as poverty, limited English proficiency, racial minority group membership, and others, a few take the brave step of beginning to look at how the school system itself structures inequality and how school staff, school policies, school curriculum, and so on, are part of the problem. An example is Hollinger Elementary school in Arizona, where teachers worked with a group of applied anthropologists to implement an approach called "funds of knowledge." Key domains of change in this approach are as follows: "(1) the development of teachers as qualitative researchers; (2) the formation of new relationships with families; and (3) the redefinition of local households as sites containing important social and intellectual resources for teaching" (González et al., 1995, p. 445). By recasting low-income, Latino households from sites that are culturally deprived to sites where valued knowledge and skills are transmitted from one generation to the next, González and her colleagues fundamentally shifted the way we think about schools and communities. Another example of schools seeking to examine their own part in creating student failure are those that try to eliminate or reduce tracking. Recognizing that the practice of grouping students by presumed ability has resulted in low-ability and high-ability tracks that too often become permanent pathways with no exit, "detracking" schools are moving toward less rigid and hierarchical grouping practices, high academic standards for all students, and the provision of supports that enable all students to reach their highest potential (Oakes, Wells, & Associates, 1996).

In the process of reaching this understanding that the structures, policies, and practices of school systems often create or reinforce existing societal inequalities, schools may question specifically how they help or hinder the development of positive intergroup relations. Given that the society in which U.S. schools are nested has a historical legacy of racism that still affects us today (Banks, 1997; Sleeter, 1991), schools are in a position to reinforce racial and ethnic inequality and stereotyping, which are primary causes of racial and ethnic conflict (Kreisberg, 1998). Schools can also ignore racial inequality and stereotyping or take actions to counter them. The nature of schools as partially bounded cultures within the larger national culture gives them this potential to shape a particular, local culture that may deviate somewhat from the norms and practices of the larger society. In a volume appropriately titled *Shaping School Culture: The Heart of Leadership,* Deal and Peterson (1999) pointed out that school cultures are "shaped by the ways principals, teachers, and key people reinforce, nurture, or transform underlying norms, beliefs, and assumptions" (p. 4).

If we want all children to grow and learn to their fullest potential, then certain basic elements have to be in place in schools. Children who feel physically unsafe because of threats of violence, or who constantly fear verbal abuse such as racial slurs or mockery of their language, are not going to be ready to learn (Bolman & Deal, 1991; Maslow, 1954; Norte, in press). Schools that do not safeguard these basic human needs place children at great risk of school failure. For this reason, it is vital that we consider what schools can do to constructively alter the societal conditions of racial inequality and stereotyping, to nurture a positive racial and ethnic identity among students as well as adults, and to create a strong sense of shared community in which differences are respected and valued.

Several models have been proposed in the literature for the enhancement of interethnic relations. The first of these is Allport's (1954) equal status contact theory, which asserts that positive intergroup relations will develop when the following conditions are present: (a) Groups have equal status within the context, (b) there is one-to-one personal interaction among individuals of different groups, (c) cooperative activities encourage people to work together on superordinate tasks, and (d) there is explicit support for and modeling of intergroup relations by relevant authority figures.

Building on and extending Allport's (1954) theory, Fine, Weis, and Powell (1998) wrote about three high schools that ranged along a "continuum from desegregated but racially separate to integrated communities of difference" (p. 248). However, Fine et al. found equal status contact theory to be inadequate by itself to explain what they saw in the one "integrated community of difference." They suggested that in addition to Allport's four conditions, schools need to "(1) build a sense of community among students; (2) demonstrate a commitment to creative analysis of difference, power, and privilege; and (3) invest in democratic practice with youth" (p. 249).

The reasoning behind these suggestions is that, even though many schools are technically desegregated, there is also tremendous resistance to inclusion. Fine et al.

(1998) cited research by Braddock, Dawkins, and Wilson (1995), which showed that over time, sites that purportedly have equal status contact devolve into sites where inclusion and interaction barriers such as differential expectations, or subtle forms of social exclusion, counter the move toward positive intergroup relations. It is worth noting that the three conditions Fine et al. suggested are predicated on work with high school students, and that a "creative analysis of difference, power, and privilege" might look and sound quite different at the elementary level, as would an investment in "democratic practice with youth" (p. 249).

Similar conditions are part of what Tatum (in press) called the ABCs of intergroup relations: (a) affirming identity, (b) building community, and (c) cultivating student leadership. What is different in Tatum's set of conditions is the notion of affirming identity. This grows out of her understanding of the stages of racial identity development that individuals of different racial groups experience (Cross, 1978; Helms, 1990). For somewhat different reasons and at different stages, both Black and White students (and, one would assume, students of other racial and ethnic backgrounds) need to feel secure in a sense of their own racial and ethnic identity to move outward into meaningful relationships with others. A focus on affirming identity in elementary schools might, for example, include such activities as family heritage projects in which children are asked to share with the class information they have gathered from interviews with their families. A focus on building community might include class projects in which children of different ethnic backgrounds work together to solve a shared problem such as cleaning up a park near the school that has become unsafe due to drug trafficking. Cultivating student leadership at the elementary level could involve, for example, teaching students democratic leadership skills so that they can form their own student council or serve as conflict managers on the playground. Such leadership opportunities are important for all students even at the elementary level because they foster a sense of social responsibility and empowerment.

These models for the improvement of interethnic relations provide a framework that is useful in analyzing the efforts of particular schools, like Cornell Elementary.

METHOD

As noted earlier, this article is based on data collected in a larger study called Leading for Diversity, in which qualitative case studies were done of 21 schools across the United States to learn how proactive school leaders address racial and ethnic conflicts and how they develop positive interethnic relations in the school community.[2] Cornell was one of the schools in this study. I was the primary researcher responsible for collecting data at this school over a period of three semes-

---

[2]For more information about this study and its findings, see Henze et al. (1999) or visit the project Web site at www.arcassociates.org/leading

ters, from Spring 1997 through Spring 1998. Data collection included interviews with people in a variety of role groups, including teachers, administrators, students, other staff, and parents; observations of classes, meetings, assemblies, and other key events at the school; questionnaires for faculty and a group of adult community members who attended classes at the school; and documents and records that were pertinent to the study. Altogether, 40 individuals were interviewed (some of them multiple times), 6 classes and 34 other events were observed, and questionnaires were returned by 16 of 50 faculty members and 24 community members.

I analyzed these data using an agreed-on coding scheme for the larger Leading for Diversity study. We used QSR Nud*ist, a software program for qualitative analysis, to code electronically and retrieve information related to particular topics or from certain sources. I further explored the data to search for salient patterns and themes, using methods described by qualitative researchers such as Erickson (1986), Goetz and LeCompte (1984), and Miles and Huberman (1994). Finally, I compiled a case study report to summarize the findings about this school.

CORNELL AND ITS CONTEXT

Cornell Elementary, like other schools mentioned earlier, is working hard not to blame children for conditions they have no control over, and seeking instead to create a strong learning community that builds on the resources that children, families, community, and staff members bring. However, one of the issues that has perplexed and troubled the school is the tension between providing access for English language learners through native language instruction and creating positive opportunities for interaction between ethnic groups.

Cornell is situated in a low-income area of a large city in northern California. The main entrance to the school is on a quiet, tree-lined street, but another side of the school borders on a major commercial avenue lined with numerous restaurants and stores, many of which have signs in Spanish as well as English. Although the neighborhood used to be more African American, at the time of the study (1996–1998) it was predominantly Latino, with smaller numbers of African American, Southeast Asian, and White residents. With approximately 1,400 students, Cornell was the largest elementary school in the district. The physical plant consisted of the main building (built in 1939), two other one-story buildings, and numerous portable units, all linked by a large, concrete yard where students had recess and physical education. The assistant principal commented, "It's almost three different settings even though they're all connected." The large size and the three separate buildings plus the portable units all contributed to a sense of physical isolation that staff members had to work consciously to overcome.

The drabness of the large concrete yard had been brightened to some extent by colorful murals on several portable and building walls. Inside the halls, student work provided color and life for the old buildings. A large bulletin board especially for parent announcements was prominent in the main entrance, with signs in English, Spanish, and sometimes Vietnamese and Cambodian, inviting parents to upcoming events.

A major feature of Cornell's organization was its year-round schedule in which students were assigned to one of four tracks. Each track was "on" for 3 months, and then "off" for 1 month. At any given time, there were approximately 900 to 1,050 students on track and 40 teachers. Students were not tracked randomly; some of the grouping was based on language and the need to provide primary language services in the most efficient manner possible. For example, most of the Cambodian students were on the same track so that Cambodian-speaking aides could go off track at the same time, thus saving the school money. Until a few years ago, Spanish bilingual classes were all in the same two tracks, but this created a segregation problem for the school because other students were not even on site at the same time, let alone in the same classrooms.

The racial and ethnic breakdown of Cornell's student population in 1997 showed that 68% were Hispanic, 14% were Asian, 13% were African American, 2% were Filipino, 2% were Native American, 1% were White, and 1% were Pacific Islander. The majority of certified staff were White, with 26% from other racial and ethnic groups. Cornell students were considered at risk in a number of senses. Eighty-eight percent participated in the free and reduced-price lunch program; 74% had limited English proficiency; and standardized achievement test results on the Terra Nova in English (given only to fluent or native English speakers) were low in all areas. For example, among third graders, only 13% were nearing or above proficiency in reading for their grade level. The community surrounding the school faced serious problems with drugs, gang activity, and violence, making safety and security primary concerns for school staff and parents.

Despite these acknowledged factors that statistics tell us put these children at risk for educational failure (including the idea that early failure in reading begets later school failure), the school was working hard to take a different view of the children it served, one not based on a deficit model, but rather on a view that builds on the resources children and their families bring to school.

Meeting the Need for Access to the Core Curriculum

For immigrant children with limited English proficiency, Cornell provided three types of classes: Spanish bilingual, Vietnamese bilingual, and sheltered. The Spanish bilingual classes, which served the majority of children at Cornell, were designed as a transitional program in which native language instruction was provided in the content areas to allow children to keep up with subject matter while they were acquiring English. Spanish-speaking children were first taught to read in Spanish, and English reading was added after they had begun to read comfortably in Spanish. In Cornell's program, once children made the transition to English, their Spanish literacy skills were not maintained. According to the principal, "We'd like to have maintenance or two-way [bilingual education] in the future, but can't do it all at once. ... We haven't got our literacy in English together yet." Several teachers also mentioned wishing the school could have a two-way, Spanish–English immersion program, but cited the overwhelming numbers of Spanish speakers compared to the few native or fluent English speakers as a reason why such a program could not work at Cornell.

In addition to the Spanish bilingual classes, there were also two Vietnamese bilingual classes. These classes, unlike the Spanish bilingual classes, included a few African American students. The teacher conducted class in both English and Vietnamese, but she did not teach Vietnamese literacy. All written work was done in English.

For children who were already fluent in English or for whom bilingual classes were not available because there was no credentialed teacher who spoke their language, the school provided sheltered classes. These were the most ethnically mixed of any classrooms at Cornell, typically including Cambodian, Mien, Lao, Latino, and African American students. Instruction was conducted in English by teachers who had received or were working on their Crosscultural, Language and Academic Development certificates, which prepared teachers to make instruction comprehensible by using a variety of techniques including many visuals, hands-on activities, and preorganizers. Instructional assistants who spoke the native languages of the students were available to support the English language learners.

There were only two classrooms at Cornell that were designated as "English only"—that is, neither bilingual nor sheltered. These classes included primarily African Americans and a few other students who were either native speakers of English or proficient enough to be classified as fluent.

The intent behind this array of instructional options was to provide access to the core curriculum for all students, regardless of language background. Consistent with *Lau v. Nichols* (1973), federal law requires that students not be precluded from access to the curriculum, and schools therefore must find ways to provide such access, whether through native language instruction, sheltering strategies, or other combinations. The federal law did not mandate a certain type of program, and states have interpreted the federal law in a variety of ways. California at one time had a law that required transitional bilingual instruction if a school had a certain number of students of similar age who all spoke the same native language. However, that law "sunsetted" in 1987, and from 1987 to 1998, schools had only to follow the federal mandate to provide access, but were free to choose any method of providing access. Since 1998, with the passage of Proposition 227, bilingual instruction has been outlawed in California and can only be offered if a majority of parents at a school sign waivers requesting it. Parents at Cornell did this, and thus bilingual education continues there to date.

Multiple Intentions, Conflicting Means

If the only intent at Cornell were to provide access to the core curriculum, things would be simpler, although not necessarily better for children. However, like most educators, the leadership and staff at Cornell envisioned their school serving multiple goals, only one of which was to provide equal access to curriculum. Another important goal was to teach students to respect others, and within that to value individual, cultural, and other differences. This goal was reflected in the school's motto, "Respect, literacy, and lifelong learning." As the principal explained it,

> Basically, there's sort of different layers about how we're proactive about dealing with different kinds of issues. I think the most broad layer that exists is our mission statement and the philosophy of respect. Our whole school motto is respect, literacy, and lifelong learning. So we basically put respect first as the condition that we like to create around us, that would be like the air we breathe. So that under the issue of respect comes all things that are related to interactions. Of course, a lot of them are overtly or covertly related to issues of ethnicity and culture. When we do that, that becomes a backdrop to refer to if someone makes a [racially stereotyping] comment.

However, developing this respect and the valuing of differences was seen as problematic given the way the school was structured around the delivery of bilingual services.[3] A teacher of a fourth- and fifth-grade sheltered class commented, "We've known for a long time that our kids are basically segregated by language, which ends up being segregated racially or culturally." Another teacher who taught a Spanish bilingual fourth- and fifth-grade class said,

> All my Spanish-speaking kids stay together as one cluster and know nothing about anybody else at the school, even though we're a really rich and diverse school and everything else. To them all the Asians are Chinese, and all the Blacks are scary and that's pretty much the picture they leave here with.

As this bilingual teacher noted, the segregation of her Spanish-speaking students from the rest of the school population contributed to their tendency to stereotype other students. Because they had little day-to-day interaction with Asian and African American students that might lead to a more complicated recognition of their

---

[3]It is important to note that bilingual education, in and of itself, does not have to mean segregating children by language. In fact, some of the most successful bilingual programs are those that follow a two-way immersion model, where two groups of students learn each other's languages (Genesee, 1999).

identity, they relied on images they had gathered from home, television, and playground gossip.

In my interviews with several fourth- and fifth-grade students, I heard firsthand evidence of this tendency to stereotype other ethnic groups. For example, one group of students who served as conflict managers were trying to answer my question about the ethnicity of other conflict managers. A student volunteered the information that there was a Chinese conflict manager. A second student countered, "She isn't Chinese." I asked, "What is she then?" The second student replied, "She's, like, Vietnamese." A third student said, "That's just like Chinese." None of the students countered this seemingly authoritative statement. Later in the same interviews, several of the students used the term *chinks* to refer to Asian students. One of the conflict managers, a Cambodian boy, also shared his painful experience of hearing other children on the playground mocking his language by making sounds that were supposed to imitate it.

The principal also recognized the inherent tension between the bilingual program and the goal of integration:

> One of the limitations of a bilingual program is that some of the kids aren't as integrated as one might hope, because of the language needs. We've done some things to remedy it, but there's always a sense that it's not enough and sort of a tension between the need to do a bilingual program in the primary language and the need to integrate children. And probably the different people you talk to would line up on bilingual issues differently. And some might see it as a big problem and then it is a catch-22, because not having bilingual education is a racist stand, too. Some people who aren't in favor of it might not perceive it that way, but in my view bilingual education is an equity issue. So those things are juxtaposed.

Her point is well taken. Many people might assume that if segregation results from the way the bilingual program is structured, schools ought to do away with bilingual education. However, not providing children with access to the core curriculum is tantamount to denying them an education, an equally racist stance. Well-implemented bilingual programs allow children who are not yet proficient in the dominant language to have access to the curriculum and to maintain their native language while they are learning English. They also build in opportunities for interaction across language groups.

Building Positive Interethnic Relations: At the Margins, in the Center, and Beyond the School

As the principal noted, the school leadership team had "done some things to remedy" the segregation produced by the particular way the bilingual program was set up. However, given that students spent about 80% of the day in their core classrooms, many of these remedies were relegated to the other 20% of the time. If we think of the center of the school day as being the activity setting in which students spend the bulk of their time, then the core classrooms where students are instructed in reading, math, language arts, science, and social studies form this center, and the other activity settings in which students do electives, after-school activities, lunch-time, recess activities, and assemblies form the margins of the school day. Al-though these activities are important in students' lives, it is also clear that, from the perspective of those who control education (e.g., district administrators, state legis-lators), the core curriculum is what really matters. In the next sections, I describe some of the key efforts staff at Cornell were making to develop positive interethnic relations.

At the Margins

Assemblies and other special events with an ethnic or multicultural focus. Cornell staff made a big effort to celebrate all the cultures of the students who attended, although at times culture was still understood in stereotypical and overly generalized ways. Throughout the year, assemblies and special events were held that highlighted one or several cultures or ethnic groups. The intent of these as-semblies was to produce positive effects on cross-cultural understanding, tolerance of differences, and respect for one's own and other cultures. The range of assem-blies and special events was quite large, including some that were not focused on specific ethnic groups. Those that were observed included National Day of Preven-tion of Gun Violence, during which students learned a pledge: "If I see a gun, I will not touch it and I will tell an adult about it"; a talent show, in which students from all classes in Grades 3 through 5 performed, most with an ethnic or cultural focus; a fire safety assembly; a Chinese New Year celebration; an African American Shake-spearean group; an oratorical fest for Black History Month; a kite festival; an Asian American assembly; a Native American assembly; and a very large *Cinco de Mayo* fair that took up a whole day and involved the entire community.

Unlike some schools, Cornell's ethnic assemblies were not restricted to a particu-lar ethnic group. Staff members encouraged students of any ethnic group to perform. Thus, in a fourth-grade Cambodian dance performance, several African American students performed alongside Cambodian students. When I asked one of the African American boys later if he had chosen on his own to be part of that performance, he as-sured me he had and that he did it because it seemed like "it would be fun." This par-ticular performance, it should be noted, was the work of a sheltered classroom with a broad mix of students. The dance performance gave them an opportunity to show-case relationships that had been developed throughout the year.

There was, however, a problematic side to the assemblies and the planning that went into them. Beneath the overt intention of celebrating cultures and appreciating differences lay old animosities among the staff and community. The tradition- ally large *Cinco de Mayo* event was perceived by some as favoring Latinos. Teachers eventually voted to do away with this celebration and instead have a large multicultural festival on July 4, with shorter celebrations taking place for specific cultures throughout the year. However, several Latino parents later argued against this change, and the issue went up for a vote among the grade-level circuits. Cinco de Mayo was restored, but resentments continued to simmer among those faculty members who had tried to create what they considered a more multicultural and equal-status array of special events. The principal was keenly aware of these tensions and tried hard to mediate and mollify them whenever possible:

> They were saying, "You only care about Latinos and you don't do enough for Asians." When the truth was it had to do with the committee, at least in my perception, and who came forward. So what I did last year, was that the African American parents came forward to do a bunch of special things and Latinos in the community came for- ward. And so instead of eliminating stuff to keep it balanced, I came and just used re- sources to bring in an Asian dance group. I think we ended up with an Asian dance group, a Karate demonstration also from Chinese martial arts. ... My personal goal is to balance the inequities that I see ... without having to go through any big committee. ... No one's going to argue with those activities. It doesn't take anyone's time. The kids have fun things and I'll make those kind of representative. ... I want to get us out of that hurt feeling.

Another problematic side to the assemblies, mentioned by many staff members, was their tendency to be piecemeal and superficial. There was little follow-up treatment of the assembly topics in classrooms. Sleeter (1991) pointed out that the assembly route is often the first pathway a school takes toward becoming more "multicultural": "Many well-intentioned but superficial school practices parade as multicultural education, such as food fairs, costume shows, and window dressing contributions by people of color" (p. 9). At Cornell, although assemblies were cer- tainly not the only efforts to be multicultural, they were probably among the first, and as such they carried with them the history of tensions around inequality among the different ethnic groups.

After-school programs and other opportunities for students to mix.

Recognizing that segregation was a problem during 80% of the school day, Cornell staff had decided to capitalize as much as possible on the remaining 20% of the day as an opportunity for children to engage in mixed-group activities. These included after-school activities such as *Capoeira,* Boy Scouts, Brownies, and *Baile Folklorico,* as well as school-related activities such as serving on student council, being a conflict manager, or being a student assistant. Each year, there was also a week-long trip for the older grades to a nearby national park. Although the focus of these activities was not interethnic relationship building, they did in some cases function as a forum for children of different ethnicities to mix and get to know one another. Those that were not mixed were the result of parent requests that the school wanted to honor (e.g., *Baile Folklorico* and a Vietnamese literacy class).

Physical education and organized sports activities during lunchtime recess were another way in which cross-group relationship building was promoted. The physical education teacher believed that by stressing the need for everyone to share the same set of rules, "you eliminate a lot of the bullying and break up cliques."

Staff members who commented on the impact of these opportunities confirmed much of what Allport's (1954) equal status contact theory suggests. The after-school coordinator reflected, "When kids have opportunities to engage in meaningful stuff with kids of other races—projects, capoeira, student council, working to plan stuff—that's the best way to get them to know each other." A teacher said, "One time when the kids really mix a lot is during the trip to [the national park]. I've seen friendships made in that week because they are with each other 24 hours a day. I've seen people who never mixed before, mixing."

Despite these positive effects, as one teacher noted, "The language issues still tend to separate people because the language you speak will determine who you play with." Thus even when settings are designed to have students of many ethnic groups participating, communication needs may overshadow the integrative desires of the adults who direct the activities. My observations in the school suggest that students were most likely to interact with students of other ethnicities when activities were structured in such a way that they had to communicate across ethnic boundaries to get the task or game done.

In the Center

Several efforts to promote positive interethnic relations were designed to be more in the center of the school day. These included the Tribes and Conflict Resolution (CR) programs, efforts to recruit diverse staff, professional development that focused on equity and intergroup relations, and a unique example of teaming between two classrooms.

Tribes and CR. Tribes is a national program designed for elementary schoolchildren to develop social skills and build positive relationships (Gibbs, 1995). Although it is usually referred to as a program, it is actually curriculum based, with a manual of lessons to be integrated into the classroom on a regular basis. At the time the study began, Tribes had been used at Cornell for 10 years. Thus it had a long history and was well embedded in the practices of the school at all levels. The principal credited Tribes with developing

> a philosophy of acceptance and intercultural understanding and communication and using "I messages" and listening to each other and appreciation. And all that stuff really makes a big difference, because we have tools to use when stuff comes up.

The Tribes community agreements or norms were posted in the staff lounge and in most classrooms. They were: (a) attentive listening, (b) appreciation/no put downs, (c) the right to pass, and (d) mutual respect. According to the chief executive officer of the company that publishes Tribes materials, "It doesn't address racial conflict directly, but changes the environment in the school so that there isn't any." One of the first Cornell teachers to be trained in Tribes stated, "While Tribes does not explicitly teach about stereotyping or prejudice, the Tribes process should be in place before one attempts to teach this sensitive topic" (Gibbs, 1995, p. 133). At Cornell, Tribes was often cited as the structure within which a racial discussion could take place. During my research at the school, I saw many examples of the Tribes norms in use in staff interactions as well as with students. Many staff members and students told me that conflict and violence had dropped in the past few years due to the combination of Tribes and CR.

Cornell began its CR program (Community Boards of San Francisco, 1987) in 1987. Thus at the time of the study it had been in operation 12 years. Like the Tribes training, every teacher at Cornell had to be trained in CR. There were two components to the program—a curriculum-based program that teachers were supposed to weave into their core classrooms and training for student conflict managers in Grades 3 through 6. The conflict managers checked in with a teacher once a week to discuss any problems they were having, as well as their successes. Parent workshops were held in all the languages spoken by families at the school to tell them about the CR program.

Like Tribes, the CR program was not explicit about racial and ethnic tensions as a potential source of conflict. In other words, it was not built into the training for either adults or children. Several staff members said, "If it comes up, we deal with it" using the CR process. On the other hand, conflict managers were told to go to an adult if certain kinds of conflict came to their attention, including "anything physical, any kind of sexual harassment, anything racial, and anything about money." The staff encouraged a range of students to become conflict managers, including students of different ethnic groups, different English language abilities, different academic achievement levels, and "kids who are troublemakers and leaders among their peers." Thus student conflict managers were able to play roles as leaders that were not dependent on grades or language proficiency.

Although Tribes and CR were viewed very positively by most staff members and students, they were also problematic in a few ways. First, there appeared to be confusion about the expected outcomes of Tribes processes. A parent coordinator said she thought the program was supposed to make kids respectful of others' feelings via "I messages" and other techniques. However, "if it was working, you'd see a better environment." I later checked out this critique with a teacher who used Tribes frequently. He responded that the "I messages" used in Tribes were not intended to change people or make them behave differently. The point is simply to share one's feelings. He felt that, for this purpose, "I messages" were very effective.

Several teachers pointed out that Tribes and CR were limited by a lack of reinforcement in the home and community. In other words, they worked well for some children, but not for those whose parents had different cultural ways of handling discipline:

> Some parents believe in using the standard discipline format as opposed to speaking to their children or taking away a privilege. So the cultural differences are still there, which make it very difficult to build on something like TRIBES. So kids get one idea here and then their home environment does not support it. If anything, it contradicts it.

One teacher also wondered whether Tribes and CR might "mask some underlying tensions—you know, because we have this in place, it tends to be either cover or shadow feelings about other groups that students might have."

Students who were conflict managers said that they were frustrated by the fact that they did not get to deal with "big" conflicts. They felt most of the conflicts they dealt with were "stupid" or "little." The implication was that they felt their work was not important because they were not solving major conflicts. They also explained that sometimes CR was used as an excuse to get out of class, and that at times, conflict managers themselves became jealous of one another and fought. They felt that because they were conflict managers, they should model conflict-free interaction, but this ideal was difficult to achieve.

Efforts to recruit diverse staff.   Cornell had a diverse staff if one looked across all different adult role groups. However, if one only looked at the credentialed teaching staff, it was still mostly White and female (74%), like most schools. The principal, a White woman, explained that, "Even though I've been limited by my possibilities, it's been a goal whenever possible. So I'm aware of it each year, when we're dealing with it." The principal spoke of consciously trying to make the staff as diverse as possible, for example, by hiring bilingual teachers who were actually native speakers of Spanish. However, given the pool of teacher candidates willing to teach in low-income, urban schools, attracting teachers was always an issue.

The instructional assistants mirrored the student population to a much larger extent than the teachers did. Cornell also had a unique program called Academic Mentors. The 10 mentors were paid out of Title VII funds to provide additional support to students at risk. They carried out a variety of reading support activities, as well as lunchtime activities. Three of the mentors were African American and seven were Latina. Several were parents or grandparents of children at the school. Having adult role models who lived in the neighborhood and were from cultural backgrounds similar to those of the students served a variety of purposes related to interethnic relations, not the least of which was encouraging underperforming students to do better academically, as an instructional assistant pointed out:

> When you can relate to the student, they act better and do better. ... Bilingual teachers who are not Latina, they can do a good job, too. But they have to really think and learn a lot about the culture. Where[as] Latino teachers, they know how to get to the kids.

Diverse staff members who worked together on shared projects also modeled positive interethnic relations for students. The two parent coordinators, one Latina and one African American, organized many activities together and in doing so, demonstrated the value and utility of interethnic alliances. In classrooms, non-White teachers and instructional assistants provided feedback to students when racially derogatory comments were made, feedback that was qualitatively different from that provided by White teachers, who also admonished students who made racial slurs. Staff members of color were able to speak personally about the racism they experienced to communicate to students how it feels, as a Korean American teacher explained:

> There's a stereotype among the Spanish-speaking community that all Asians are Chinese. ... And it really upsets me, and then I think, we could help in that area. ... If I hear someone saying it, I'll bring it up and say, "you know, I really resent that because ... all Asians are not Chinese. ... " I'll say that publicly, "It's very insulting and it's a put down and I would really appreciate your not making that generalization. You know, it's like saying all Spanish speaking students are Mexican." I always pose it that way. Now a lot of where they hear that from is the parents, so we have to educate our parents, too.

A problem in the profile of Cornell's diverse staff was that most of the non-White staff members had lower levels of education and less power and status at the school. Few of the instructional assistants and other noncredentialed staff of color would attend faculty meetings because these meetings were held after their paid time, whereas faculty were paid to attend. A structure that countered this, however, was the Leadership Team, a site-based management team composed of 18 individuals drawn from different role groups in the school, including a classified staff representative, a parent center representative, and others. By specifically including these groups, at least some diversity was ensured within this decision-making body.

Teacher-driven professional development focused on equity.   A small group of Cornell teachers had developed a monthly forum called SEED—Seeking Educational Equity and Diversity (MacIntosh & Style, 2000). The purpose of SEED was primarily to increase teachers' awareness and to empower teachers to work together on actions they could take to work against racism, sexism, homophobia, classism, and so on. The group originated as a teacher dialogue group in 1990, focusing on Freire's (1970) ideas about critical pedagogy. Sensing a lack of direction and focus in the group, one of the teachers learned of SEED, a model of teacher change disseminated nationally by a group at Wellesley College. She received support from the Leadership Team for herself and another teacher to be trained as SEED facilitators.

The framework used in SEED consists of five stages of inclusion, from being marginal to being in the center. The five stages were related to curriculum, and teachers tried to place what they were doing in terms of what stage it looked most like. "We don't want to do the single group approach," a teacher explained, "because again, if everybody is in the center, there's no need to do these special events to make sure nobody's marginalized." One of the teacher leaders described four of the five phases:

> In Phase 1, the only relevant things that are taught are things that have been done or accomplished by White men. … In Phase 3, you have exceptional people that come from outside of the White male thing, so you'll be talking about Harriet Tubman and Martin Luther King, or whatever, but still they're marginalized because they're the exception to the norm, or they act like White men and so they're now acceptable to bring into the curriculum. In Phase 4—I think every once in a while I see examples of it happening—where, if you look in my classroom, there are things here that would be considered Phase 4, when we're looking at geography and instead of using some textbook we're using where the kids come from. So that would be a Phase 4 type thing. And then her [MacIntosh's] dream is of this Phase 5 that doesn't really exist but where everybody's in the center, where you don't have to have a women's month and you don't have to have an African American month because everyone's included all the time.

The SEED group varied in size and frequency of meetings; they had trouble finding a time to come together. Occasionally, SEED spearheaded a larger event, for example, showing the film *Color of Fear* (Stirfry Productions, 1994). That meeting was very successful, with a turnout of 40 to 50 participants. One of the reasons this meeting was so successful was, according to one teacher, because the film was somewhat known. It also did not require people to commit to coming to the group every time, and the film featured men and therefore drew more men.

For the core group of about 10 teachers who attended regularly, SEED had a powerful impact. Teachers involved with SEED also seemed to take the lead in schoolwide and across-schools change, and in political action within the community (e.g., meeting with teachers at other schools, leading action against Proposition 227). The vision of their roles as educators went beyond the classroom, and SEED had given them tools to implement that bigger vision. But it also had a direct impact on the curriculum they used in class and the way they taught. One teacher said, "SEED was the first place where I could actually seriously think about, become aware of and really start working on, things in my classroom and not just cosmetics. … SEED provides the only place to discuss hard issues." Another pointed out, "It helped legitimize what my gut was telling me I wanted to do, so now there were a lot of people out there saying, this is an OK practice, not only OK, but an exemplary type of way to teach, especially in schools like ours that are so multicultural." A third teacher said, "I became aware of prejudices I didn't know I had, and also of power issues and the damage done to minority groups."

Teaming between two classrooms.   Some teachers had chosen to try to break down the segregation of the students by teaming together, meaning that two classes (usually a bilingual, all-Latino group with a sheltered group that was a mixture of ethnicities) combined their students and did project-based work, with students collaborating in small groups of mixed ethnicities and language backgrounds. The two teachers who had implemented this model most fully were a White teacher named Sylvia and a Korean American teacher named Lenny. They were the only teachers who teamed all day long. Other teams worked together for only 1 hr a day, which was a requirement of the district. Lenny and Sylvia explained,

> One of the reasons why Sylvia and I team is that she has mainly Spanish-speaking students, and I have mainly Cambodian, and we want them to have an opportunity where they're working with other students, so they have to understand each other and know how to problem solve. (Lenny)
>
> Lenny and I do this on a very conscious level … . We let the kids know on the first day there are three reasons why we're doing this, and one of them is learning about each other and learning how to get along with each other, learning how to really respect, develop bonds with each other. And we make it a very explicit part of our curriculum. We don't just say it but we actually act on it. (Sylvia)

Most of Sylvia's students, although still considered limited English proficient, had enough fluency to understand basic English. For those who were still at a beginning level of English, she provided Spanish instruction in small groups or individually. Their model of teaming worked in part because students were at an advanced enough level of English to benefit from a project-based curriculum delivered primarily in English. On one occasion when I observed Sylvia and Lenny's combined class, there were 62 fourth- and fifth-grade students all working in small groups on an immigration project.

The students had interviewed their parents about immigration and now they were starting to pool their information into a matrix. The interview asked parents about their push and pull factors in immigration, and the matrix reflected these questions: Where did they move from and where did they move to? Why did they leave? What were they hoping to find, or do, or accomplish? How did they get there? What were the outcomes (e.g., did they accomplish what they had hoped; was it different from what they had expected)?

As each student shared his or her interview responses with the group, everyone in the group had to write down on his or her matrix what that person was sharing. In one group, an African American girl named Jamila was sharing her interview. She told the other students that her family was African American, that they had moved from a nearby city because they wanted their children to live in the city in which they currently resided, have a car, and have a better life. She felt happy because they had a better life. Other students in the group who were from Cambodia and Bosnia shared their interview results in turn. Jamila was very helpful to the rest of the team, especially helping the Bosnian girl.

Sylvia, Lenny, and other teachers and staff who were familiar with their students all saw impressive results in terms of interethnic relations that they claimed were due to the teaming structure. The after-school coordinator commented, "It's unique at this school. And some of the kids in that combined class are best friends [joined] at the hip." Sylvia herself said,

> I see incredible bonding and friendships and interactions between cultures. And the partnerships, they kind of move around a lot as that age group does, but I see so many cross cultural experiences, real ones, relationships, and hanging out at recess and lunch. I feel on that level it's definitely working.

Unfortunately, although this approach seemed to be among the most powerful in terms of breaking down racial and ethnic barriers, there were few supports for it to happen on a more schoolwide basis, and many constraints. The district did have a requirement that students had to be "integrated" 20% of the day, but this was far less than what Sylvia and Lenny were doing. Legally, they were in suspect territory because, as a teacher pointed out, "You can't [do more] because if you're meeting the bilingual requirement, you have to have primary language 80% of the time." Thus Sylvia, with her bilingual Spanish group, was actually in violation of district policy. Furthermore, even if their model were legally possible, there were not enough nonbilingual classes to have all the classrooms matched, as the principal explained: "If you have two thirds of one ethnicity and one third of the others, you can't match every class one to one."

Beyond the School: Parent Involvement

Cornell staff and leaders were making serious efforts to involve parents of diverse backgrounds in the school. These efforts, particularly when they brought parents of different ethnic groups together in an interactive format, had the potential to change attitudes in the home about other ethnic groups.

Among the various parent involvement efforts at Cornell were the Parent Center, a portable unit in the center of the yard specifically dedicated as a place where parents could come for meetings, or just to chat with a parent coordinator; a Family Resource Center, where parents and other family members could access a wide range of health and social services; translation services that were made available during most meetings and events involving parents; a Parent Education Program that included English as a second language instruction, a Spanish literacy class, a Family Stories class, and general equivalency diploma (GED) classes; a parent accountability event that over 600 parents attended to hear how students at Cornell were doing academically and to discuss ways to improve academic achievement; and responses to parent requests, such as the Vietnamese literacy class after school.

A tension that pervaded many parent involvement efforts was that although there was a sense of striving for equal outreach to all ethnic groups, when one group appeared to be getting more attention, other groups either felt shortchanged or wanted to have the same level of effort directed toward them. Another difficulty arose because of the need to provide services in the language parents could understand. As a result, some meetings were held by language group to facilitate communication and also help parents feel comfortable. This had a dual effect: It increased access for those parents, but also segregated them from other parents who had to meet separately because of their own language needs. This was essentially the same tension that pervaded the bilingual program—the tension between the two goals of providing access and creating an integrated environment. The school tried to get around this tension by doing some of both types of activities—some that were multicultural and others that were unicultural.

Probably the most in-depth cross-cultural sharing among parents took place in the parent education classes, which for the most part involved different ethnic groups and were viewed as a good way for parents to get to know one another across ethnic lines. Attendance was high and the program was well established in the life of the school. The relatively recent addition of the GED classes had helped the school reach out to African American parents, who formerly did not attend because all other classes were designed for nonnative speakers of English. The GED teacher said, "It's one of the most diverse classes I've ever taught. It's wonderful. It truly reflects the school." In the Family Stories class, parents told stories about their own lives and then, with the help of bilingual assistants, wrote the stories in their native language or English. Three books have been published as a result of this effort (Family Stories Group, 1992, 1993, 1995). In this cross-cultural context, parents explored and reflected on universal themes such as love and relationships, raising children, and immigrating to the United States. According to one parent, the classes gave "more chances to talk to each other, to know more about other groups of people. It is really helpful." Another parent, when asked whether these classes help race relations, replied, "*Yo creo que si, porque existe la comunicacion entre los grupos etnicos*" (I think so, because there is communication among the ethnic groups).

DISCUSSION: CAN SCHOOLS BE VEHICLES FOR IMPROVING INTERETHNIC RELATIONS?

With its rich tapestry of cultural traditions embedded in the student, parent, and staff populations and its rapidly shifting and ever-creative movement toward new forms of school culture, Cornell was struggling to become a place where students and adults of different ethnic and cultural groups could both find strength in their own ethnic identity and also reach out across groups to form alliances and shared community. This is not easy. Rosaldo (1989) described the dilemma facing racial minority groups in what he called "cultural border zones":

> [R]ace relations in North America involve a blend of assimilationist efforts, raw prejudice, and cultural containment that revolves around a concerted effort to keep each culture pure and in its place. Members of racial minority groups receive a peculiar message: either join the mainstream or stay in your ghettos, barrios, and reservations, but don't try to be both mobile and cultural. (p. 212)

Cornell was a site where these static categories were beginning to break down, and where, in their place, I found an energizing sense of motion. The practices and structures I have described have no doubt changed in the 2 years since I last visited, but there appears to be a constant: Cornell is a school seeking to define itself in ways that have not yet been accomplished in other places, making the process both frustrating and highly creative. Having journeyed through many dimensions of Cornell's efforts to promote positive relations among different ethnic groups, I want now to return to the question I posed at the beginning of this article: Can schools be vehicles for improving race relations?

Many would argue that, given the historical inequities that have been created and perpetuated in schools (e.g., segregation, tracking), schools are uniquely unqualified to serve as vehicles for undoing racism and ethnic conflict. When I posed the question recently in a college classroom of about 60 teacher education students, about 10 of them responded that they thought it was impossible for schools to improve race relations for the aforementioned reasons. They felt schools are too much a part of the problem to be really helpful in undoing racism and healing race relations.

In addition, it is clear that schools face "givens" that are part of the larger district, state, and national context and cannot be easily changed from within the school. Cornell faced several of these givens, including the district-imposed structure of the transitional bilingual program, the imbalance in the numbers of students of different ethnic groups attending the school, the lack of available people of color who are credentialed teachers, and the need to provide translation in parent meetings and the resulting tendency to hold those meetings by language-specific groups. Also, a powerful given in any school is the societal racism that exists in every community and filters into the school through parental attitudes, media stereotypes, and differential teacher expectations.

However, it is equally clear that teachers, both individually and in pairs or groups such as Sylvia and Lenny, can do a great deal within their classrooms to "affirm identity, build community, and cultivate student leadership" (Tatum, in press), as well as to model positive intergroup relations among adults (Allport, 1954) and "creatively analyze difference, power, and privilege" (Fine et al., 1998, p. 249). Such classrooms provide students with a "cross cultural and comparative perspective" (Gibson, 1987, p. 310) that is much needed if U.S. schools are to play a role in eliminating racial prejudice. However, these conditions must also be reflected in the larger institutional culture of the school, not in just a few classrooms but in every aspect of the school, including staffing, leadership structures and processes, curriculum and pedagogy, academic and behavioral standards, special programs, celebratory events, professional development of staff, and parent and community involvement. Cornell shows us how one school made determined efforts in all of these realms of school functioning and, as a result, was doing better in terms of ethnic relations than were many neighboring elementary schools. Yet teachers were not satisfied. Several of them, particularly those involved in SEED, thought the school still had a long way to go to become truly antiracist. They felt that multiculturalism was still practiced in largely superficial or "touristy" ways, such as focusing on foods and festivals, rather than, as the SEED framework suggests, placing everyone in the center.

Schools already do have the power to shape race relations in negative ways through sorting, tracking, unequal discipline, and silence about race. The question has to turn to whether or not they will use this power in a positive way. Cornell provides one example of how a school struggled with important priorities that placed integration at odds with bilingual education, but they still managed to work at the margins of the school day, in the center, and beyond the school to create opportunities for positive race relations to develop. To do this required awareness and strong leadership from administrators, teachers, and parent leaders who were committed to developing structures that would countervail the givens that kept people separate. In their creative resistance to racial polarization, members of the Cornell community show us how cultural production in the "borderlands" works, much as Anzaldua (1987) described the individual of mixed ancestry:

> The new *mestiza* copes by developing a tolerance for contradictions, a tolerance for ambiguity. She learns to be Indian in Mexican culture, to be Mexican from an Anglo point of view. She learns to juggle cultures. She has a plural personality, she operates in a pluralistic mode. … Not only does she sustain contradictions, she turns the ambivalence into something else. (p. 79)

ACKNOWLEDGMENTS

This study was funded through two grants, one through the Field Initiated Studies program (PR R308F60028), and another through the Center for Research on Education, Diversity and Excellence (PR R306A60001). Both grants are administered by the Office of Educational Research and Improvement (OERI), U.S. Department of Education (USDOE).

I wish to thank the staff, students, and parents at Cornell for sharing with me their efforts to make the school a positive, safe, and respectful place for learning.

The content, findings, and opinions expressed here are those of the author and do not necessarily represent the positions or policies of OERI or USDOE.

REFERENCES

Allport, G. (1954). *The nature of prejudice.* Cambridge, MA: Addison-Wesley.

Anzaldua, G. (1987). *Borderlands/la frontera: The new mestiza.* San Francisco: Spinsters/Aunt Lute.

Banks, J. (1997). *Teaching strategies for ethnic studies* (6th ed.). Boston: Allyn & Bacon.

Bolman, L., & Deal, T. (1991). *Reframing organizations.* San Francisco: Jossey-Bass.

Braddock, J., Dawkins, M., & Wilson, P. (1995). Intercultural contact and race relations among American youth. In D. W. Hawley & A. W. Jackson (Eds.), *Toward a common destiny: Improving race and ethnic relations in America* (pp. 237–256). San Francisco: Jossey-Bass.

Community Boards of San Francisco. (1987). *Conflict resolution: An elementary school curriculum.* San Francisco: Author.

Cross, W. E. (1978). The Cross and Thomas models of psychological nigrescence. *Journal of Black Psychology, 5*(1), 13–19.

Deal, T., & Peterson, K. (1999). *Shaping school culture: The heart of leadership.* San Francisco: Jossey-Bass.

Erickson, F. (1986). Qualitative methods in research on teaching. In M. Wittrock (Ed.), *Handbook of research on teaching* (3rd ed., pp. 119–161). New York: Collier Macmillan.

Family Stories Group. (1992). *Our stories, our lives [Nuestras historias, nuestras vidas]* (Vol. 1). Oakland, CA: ARC Associates.

Family Stories Group. (1993). *Our stories, our lives [Nuestras historias, nuestras vidas]* (Vol. 2). Oakland, CA: ARC Associates.

Family Stories Group. (1995). *Our stories, our lives [Nuestras historias, nuestras vidas]* (Vol. 3). Oakland, CA: ARC Associates.

Fine, M., Weis, L., & Powell, L. (1998). Communities of difference: A critical look at desegregated spaces created for and by youth. *Harvard Educational Review, 67,* 247–284

Freire, P. (1970). *Pedagogy of the oppressed.* New York: Continuum.

Genesee, F. (Ed.). (1999). *Program alternatives for linguistically diverse students* (CREDE Educational Practice Rep. No. 1). Washington, DC: Center for Applied Linguistics.

Gibbs, J. (1995). *Tribes: A new way of learning and being together.* Sausalito, CA: Center Source Systems.

Gibson, M. (1987). Punjabi immigrants in an American high school. In G. Spindler & L. Spindler (Eds.), *Interpretive ethnography of education at home and abroad* (pp. 281–312). Hillsdale, NJ: Lawrence Erlbaum Associates, Inc.

Goetz, J., & LeCompte, M. (1984). *Ethnography and qualitative design in educational research.* Orlando, FL: Academic.

González, N., Moll, L., Floyd-Tenery, M., Rivera, A., Rendon, P., Gonzales, R., & Amanti, C. (1995). Funds of knowledge for teaching in Latino households. *Urban Education, 29,* 443–470.

Helms, J. E. (Ed). (1990). *Black and White racial identity: Theory, research, and practice.* Westport, CT: Greenwood.

Henze, R., Katz, A., Norte, E., Sather, S., & Walker, E. (1999). *Leading for diversity: A study of how school leaders achieve racial and ethnic harmony* (Final rep.). Oakland, CA: ARC Associates.

Kozol, J. (1991). *Savage inequalities: Children in America's schools.* New York: Crown.

Kreisberg, L. (1998). *Constructive conflicts: From escalation to resolution.* Lanham, MD: Rowman & Littlefield.

Lau v. Nichols, 414 U.S. 563, 566 (1973).

MacIntosh, P., & Style, E. (2000). *The SEED project on inclusive curriculum.* Retreived May 24, 2000, from the World Wide Web: http://www.wellesley.edu/WCW/projects/seed.html

Maslow, A. (1954). *Motivation and personality.* New York: Harper & Row.

McDermott, R., & Varenne, H. (1995). Culture as disability. *Anthropology and Education Quarterly, 26,* 324–348.

Miles, M., & Huberman, M. (1994). *Qualitative data analysis* (2nd ed.). Thousand Oaks, CA: Sage.

Norte, E. (in press). Structures "beneath the skin": How school leaders use their power and authority to create institutional opportunities for developing positive interethnic communities. *Journal of Negro Education.*

Oakes, J., Wells, A. S., & Associates. (1996). *Beyond the technicalities of school reform: Policy lessons from detracking schools.* Los Angeles: University of California, Los Angeles, Graduate School of Education and Information Studies.

Rosaldo, R. (1989). *Culture and truth: The remaking of social analysis.* Boston: Beacon.

Sleeter, C. (1991). Introduction: Multicultural education and empowerment. In C. Sleeter (Ed.), *Empowerment through multicultural education* (pp. 1–23). Albany: State University of New York Press.

Stirfry Productions. (1994). *The color of fear* [video]. Oakland, CA: Author.

Tatum, B. (in press). Commentary. *Journal of Negro Education.*

JOURNAL OF EDUCATION FOR STUDENTS PLACED AT RISK, 6(1&2), 157–159

COMMENTARIES

The Holographic Properties of Diversity

Gil N. Garcia

Office of Educational Research and Improvement
U.S. Department of Education

When diversity works, the benefits to children and youth, to the schools they ultimately attend, and to their homes and communities are significant. The concept and its many practice iterations do indeed provide the structures and support that appear necessary to build and sustain the attitudes, self-esteem, and aptitude necessary for adults to teach effectively and, by extension, for children and youth to meet high learning expectations. In short, diversity is a useful tool.

Regrettably, as described in most of the education research literature, diversity remains too loosely interpreted. It can simply be a policy statement that recognizes racial, ethnic, gender, and social class differences among students. It can also be a declaration that such differences will be respected. Furthermore, diversity issues are too casually implemented and evaluated. Thus, it is difficult to determine their effects on teaching and on learning. Worse yet, the issues that define diversity are frequently placed in separate boxes or treated as separate program components.

It is thus refreshing to read the papers that make up this special issue. Collectively, the authors highlight a host of important factors related to diversity education and to a range of activities through which the featured communities of learners help each other achieve their high expectations. The authors highlight particular concerns that need to be tended to and strategies that work. Thus, they describe organizations and programs that expressly serve as bridges among homes, schools, and communities; the value added by the services they provide; efforts across time

Requests for reprints should be sent to Gil N. Garcia, U.S. Department of Education, Office of Educational Research and Improvement, 555 New Jersey Avenue, NW, Room 611B, Washington, DC 20208. E-mail: gil_Garcia@ed.gov

and space used to gauge changes at the institutional and the personal levels; and the effects of diversity education initiatives on students, their homes, and the schools they attend. Individually, they explore these factors in great depth and care in a wide range of settings. The researchers' common strength is that they are bound by an ethic that motivates them to conduct useful research. The featured projects are helping students, their parents and family circles, school staff, and other important players. They also facilitate a better understanding of the complexities of schools and schooling. Moreover, they link institutional complexities to the role that parents play and the tasks of growing up that students must face.

The richness of the art and practice of diversity is seen in other arenas from which educators can draw lessons. Delving outside of the education box reveals diversity's other multi-dimensional qualities. Consider, for example, what diversity has begun to mean in the world of corporate business. Although interpreted and used as variously as in the field of education, in the business arena, diversity might define an initiative used to attract the right kind of worker. It might also define efforts to retain highly competitive employees who are inclined to go where the grass is greener. More and more, such initiatives also mean that managers invite employees to seek professional development to increase expertise that will help a worker—and the company—to do a better job and to increase profits. In short, diversity displays its holographic properties in varied ways and in varied circumstances.

Dell and Pfizer Corporations are but two examples of companies that have instituted very strong diversity policies and practices. On the surface, they each target particular national events or geographic regions to ensure that a wide variety of job candidates learn about them. They also ensure that their workforce is indeed ethnically, racially, and gender diverse. However, they intentionally look for different types of personalities to suit their many work niches, from product development to marketing. They also have implemented mentoring programs to teach new hires the ropes and to promote their careers in relation to their skills and expectations. In short, the diversity initiatives of these two companies are designed expressly to attract and keep the best and to promote a community spirit. Finally, their outreach efforts are neither accidental nor poorly planned. Managers mean to make their companies the best and the most competitive by whatever means.

Imagine the school district that instituted such policies. We might see the following statement: "It is the policy of this school district to ensure that we attract and sustain a workforce and student body that is well trained. If you come, we will serve you—whatever it takes. If you accept, you promise to do your best. Your achievements are our profits."

The policy would mean that parents and family groups, district staff at all levels, and students—in other words, everybody—would be involved in the process of developing school reform plans in relation to community needs and expectations; the screening and hiring of staff in relation to the goals of the reforms; and the diagnosis and assessment of students in relation to their needs, interests, and aspirations. It would give new meaning to the phrase "we're building new bridges toward the future."

The reality is that the dimensions, activities, and effects of diversity could and should be quite varied, adapting to circumstances in the same sense that a hologram's appearance changes according to its position in the light and the position of the viewer. The boundaries of creativity are person-made. Kudos to the authors!

JOURNAL OF EDUCATION FOR STUDENTS PLACED AT RISK, 6(1&2), 161–168

Building Bridges of Home, School, and Community: The Importance of Design

Joyce L. Epstein

Center on School, Family, and Community Partnerships
Johns Hopkins University

Where do children learn and grow? At home. At school. In the community. It is simply a social fact that youngsters learn from their families, teachers, peers, relatives, part-time employers, and other adults in the community. Students develop in all three contexts simultaneously and continuously. Thus, the bridges of home, school, and community are inevitably interconnected. Students travel back and forth across these bridges for many years to learn who they are and where they are going.

The success or failure of all bridges—real or symbolic—is in their design. Bridges that connect home, school, and community may be well or poorly designed. Therefore, it is important to learn about the most effective structures, processes, and practices that will produce good connections and positive results. The articles in this special issue contribute several cross-cutting conclusions that should strengthen the design of school, family, and community partnerships.

1. Families care about their children's success, but most parents need more and better information from schools and communities to become and remain productively involved in their children's education

It is important, but no longer surprising, to learn that just about all parents care about their children's progress and success in school. This includes parents with

---

Requests for reprints should be sent to Joyce Epstein, Center on School, Family, and Community Partnerships, Johns Hopkins University, 3003 North Charles Street, Suite 200, Baltimore, MD 21218. E-mail: jepstein@csos.jhu.edu

low incomes, less formal education, and those who do not speak English or read it
well (see Adger, 2001/this issue; Collignon, Men, & Tan, 2001/this issue). The
myth of parental indifference has been debunked in study after study in this and
other nations (Chavkin, 1993; Epstein & Sanders, 1998). Presently, however, only
some families are well informed and productively involved in their children's education. Parents' near-universal interest in their children's success should compel
research and practice to address the question of how to design and implement partnership programs that will help all parents use their strengths, time, and talents to
ensure their children's success in school.

2. Students learn more than academic skills at home, at school, and in the community

Students' success in school and in life is measured by many indicators, including,
but not limited to, achievement test scores. Adger's (2001/this issue) study reminds
us that student attendance, homework completion, report card grades, leadership
skills, course credits, and postsecondary educational plans are important indicators
of student success. All of these variables can be positively influenced by parents,
peers, teachers, and others in the community if activities are designed to mobilize
their support and action on these goals.

3. Students are influenced positively or negatively by their peers, by their families, and by the organization of activities in their schools and classrooms

Azmitia and Cooper (2001/this issue) showed that most White and Latino students
see their peers and friends as companions, but only some have friends who are serious about schoolwork and problem solving. Gándara, Gutiérrez, and O'Hara
(2001/this issue) studied Latino and White students in urban and rural schools.
They concluded that the students' geographic locations explained their behavior
more than did their ethnicity; that is, urban students differed from rural students,
whether White or Latino.

Importantly, these articles confirm that even as students' time with peers in-
creases across grades, parents remain important influences in their children's
lives on academic decisions about schoolwork, behaviors, and postsecondary
plans. Parents, community leaders, teachers, and other adults may serve as important counterpoints to friends and peers who challenge or distract students
from learning.

Other studies also report that students who feel connected to their families are
less likely than other adolescents to engage in risky behavior (Resnick et al.,

1997). Because school is a big part of children's lives, parents can remain connected only if they exchange useful information with educators every year about school programs, children's progress, academic decisions, and other school matters. These connections are the reason for designing programs of productive partnerships.

Henze's (2001/this issue) main question also concerns the interactions of peers and friends in school: Can school organization of specific activities promote positive intergroup relations among students with different abilities and diverse racial and ethnic backgrounds? Her case study shows how one elementary school designed activities to encourage interactions among diverse students. In this school, students were separated by ability and language in their core classes for 80% of the school day. Nevertheless, one team of teachers brought two classes of diverse students together for academic work. In addition, the school organized electives, after-school programs, lunch, recess, assemblies, and other activities to increase interactions of diverse students to try to improve race relations, reduce intergroup conflict, and increase interethnic friendships. Although the case study school has a long way to go, it is clear that, by design, school and classroom organization and activities can affect peer interactions and student behaviors. In addition, it also is imperative to bring diverse groups of parents together to create a unified school community.

These exploratory studies should encourage renewed interest in research on peer group processes in school and community contexts. The researchers identify several variables that may affect patterns of peer influence, including location (urbanicity), gender, poverty, ethnicity, risky behavior, homework habits, school and classroom organization, attitudes toward school, and family interactions. The full constellation of variables should be analyzed in studies with larger samples, longitudinal data, and within-group analyses to isolate the effects of home, school, and community on peer interaction, the selection of friends, and the influence of friends and peers on important attitudes, behaviors, and achievements (see earlier research by Epstein, 1983, and recent studies by Plank, 2000, on these issues).

4. Community-based programs may support schools, assist families, and increase students' chances of success

The articles in this issue reveal three important features of successful community-based programs: essential elements, connections with schools, and high content.

Programs that include essential elements are more likely to succeed.
When a bridge is built, engineers must meet design and construction standards. So, too, partnership programs must meet high standards for design and implementation to reach all families and to help students succeed.

Adger (2001/this issue) identified several essential elements of effective community-based programs. Interestingly, colleagues and I have been measuring indicators of successful partnership programs at the school level (Sanders, 1999) and at the district and state levels (Epstein, Clark, & Van Voorhis, 2000). Adger's and our studies identify many of the same important program components including teamwork, time, adequate budgets and other resources, goal-oriented plans tailored to the needs of the participants, strong internal and external support, and ongoing evaluations.

With a growing consensus about these basic program components, new questions should be asked about the details of each essential element. For example, cash-strapped schools and school districts want to know the minimum budgets needed to support staff and activities for high-quality partnership programs (e.g., see Epstein, Sanders, Clark, & Van Voorhis, 1999, on sources and levels of funds for effective partnership programs). Educators want to know how to attract and sustain productive community partnerships (e.g., see Sanders, in press; Sanders & Harvey, 2000). There is much to learn about the underlying details of the essential elements of partnership programs.

Community-based programs that are connected to the schools, not isolated from them, are more likely to assist families and increase student learning and success.   Sometimes community groups or leaders construct walls rather than bridges with schools (Newmann & Sconzert, 2000). Several studies in this issue indicate that students and families benefit when community-based activities are connected or complementary to the schools. For example, a community-based summer school that aims to boost student learning or an after-school tutoring program should know about the curricula, goals, and indicators on which students will be measured.

Community programs also help parents connect to their children's schools. Well-organized community-based programs may act as brokers, interpreters, and guides to help all parents, and particularly language minority families, negotiate with their children's schools (see Collignon et al., 2001/this issue; Durán, Durán, Perry-Romero, & Sanchez, 2001/this issue). Equally important, community leaders and programs can help educators understand students' families, cultures, and customs, as when families served as cultural consultants to a summer school program.

Ultimately, students must succeed in school to advance to postsecondary education, training, and employment. Therefore, educators, families, and community leaders have an obligation to talk and work together so that students benefit from all available resources and support.

Partnership programs should be goal oriented.   No one would build a bridge to nowhere. Similarly, school, family, and community partnerships need clear goals and important content. Two articles focus on the content of involvement activities that draw on family strengths and knowledge to support student learning.

Durán et al. (2001/this issue) offered a thoughtful and thorough curriculum for a community-based family literacy program that builds parents' and children's computer skills, writing skills, and interactions to produce desktop-published family stories. The study reports dramatic changes in parents' computer skills, and points to the need for future studies of program effects on students. Durán et al.'s study shows that all parents—including those who do not speak or read English—have important knowledge to share with their children if, by design, they are engaged in purposeful activities.

González, Andrade, Civil, and Moll (2001/this issue) addressed the content of partnerships with the concepts of funds of knowledge and parents' experiences with math at home (Moll, Amanti, Neff, & González, 1992). In contrast to most family involvement activities that focus on students' reading and reading-related skills, this article explores mathematics in its "natural" state, and how family knowledge in math may be used in classrooms.

Colleagues and I have been addressing a related challenge to connect students' in-school learning with families' out-of-school experiences through the design of homework. In Teachers Involve Parents in Schoolwork (TIPS), educators design interactive homework that enables all youngsters to conduct guided conversations with parents about their practical experiences in math, science, language arts, and other subjects (Epstein, Salinas, & Jackson, 1995). For example, a TIPS language arts activity may ask middle school students to write a story about someone who helped them, read the story to their family partners, and conduct a conversation with their parents about someone who helped them when they were in the middle grades. The student records the family story—a variation of the family literacy activity described by Durán et al. (2001/this issue). A TIPS math activity may guide elementary school students to show their family partners how they are learning to write fractions, and then conduct a conversation about how parents use fractions at home, much as González's examples intend to do. Because homework is assigned to all students, weekly TIPS activities reach families who are unable to attend special projects or workshops.

A DESIGN CHALLENGE: BUILD BRIDGES THAT CONNECT AND UNITE ALL PARTNERS

The overriding lesson of all of the articles in this issue is the power of design for improving programs of school, family, and community partnerships. Well-designed bridges among home, school, and community can increase student success and sustain family involvement in education across all the grades. Poorly designed bridges—or bridges unbuilt—leave students without the support they need to do their best work in school, and leave families unconnected to their children's schools.

One of the most difficult challenges in developing programs of school, family, and community partnerships is to create a unified, integrated school community for all students and families and, at the same time, assist students and families with special needs. This can be done if teachers, parents, administrators, and community partners know the families and students served by the school, work together, and write plans for partnership activities designed to meet both of these goals.

For example, all parents may be invited to an end-of-summer picnic that welcomes students and families back to school. There also may be translators at the picnic (and at all school meetings and parent–teacher conferences throughout the year) to ensure that parents who do not speak English feel welcome. During the year, Latino, Hmong, or other groups of parents may meet regularly to discuss the kinds of activities and services that would help these families boost their children's success. Their suggestions could be submitted to an action team for partnerships and considered for the school's next 1-year action plan. Without an organized team of educators and parents and systematic processes for families to influence plans for partnerships, there is likely to be the kind of bickering that Henze (2001/this issue) described if one group of families thinks it is being shortchanged in its opportunities for involvement.

Educators who are interested in building stronger bridges among home, school, and community can obtain help from the National Network of Partnership Schools at Johns Hopkins University (Epstein, Coates, Salinas, Sanders, & Simon, 1997; Sanders & Epstein, 2000; see www.partnershipschools.org). The National Network provides research-based guidelines, publications, and other tools that enable schools, districts, and state departments of education to design and maintain comprehensive programs of school, family, and community partnerships.

The articles in this issue call attention to the need for greater equity in the design and implementation of school, family, and community partnerships. Some students, including some who are at risk of failing, presently succeed in school because their parents, teachers, friends, and others in the community communicate well with each other and help students focus on their attendance, classwork, homework, and other important behaviors. More students, especially those who are at risk of failing, need this kind of coordinated support so that they, too, have a better chance to succeed in school.

REFERENCES

Adger, C. T. (2001/this issue). School–community-based organization partnerships for language minority students' school success. *Journal of Education for Students Placed At Risk, 6.*

Azmitia, M., & Cooper, C. R. (2001/this issue). Good or bad? Peer influences on Latino and White adolescents' pathways through school. *Journal of Education for Students Placed At Risk, 6.*

Chavkin, N. (Ed.). (1993). *Families and schools in a pluralistic society.* Albany: State University of New York Press.

Collignon, F., Men, M., & Tan, S. (2001/this issue). Finding ways in: Community-based perspectives on Southeast Asian family involvement with schools in a New England state. *Journal of Education for Students Placed At Risk, 6.*

Durán, R., Durán, J., Perry-Romero, D., & Sanchez, E. (2001/this issue). Latino immigrant parents and children learning and publishing together in an after-school setting. *Journal of Education for Students Placed At Risk, 6.*

Epstein, J. L. (1983). The influence of friends on achievement and affective outcomes. In J. L. Epstein & N. Karweit (Eds.), *Friends in school: Patterns of selection and influence in secondary schools* (pp. 177–200). New York: Academic.

Epstein, J. L., Clark, L. A., & Van Voorhis, F. E. (2000, April). *Three-year patterns of state and district leadership in developing programs of partnership.* Paper presented at the annual meeting of the American Educational Research Association, New Orleans, LA.

Epstein, J. L., Coates, L., Salinas, K. C., Sanders, M. G., & Simon, B. S. (1997). *School, family, and community partnerships: Your handbook for action.* Thousand Oaks, CA: Corwin.

Epstein, J. L., Salinas, K. C., & Jackson, V. (1995). *Manual for teachers: Teachers involve parents in schoolwork (TIPS) language arts, science/health, and math interactive homework in the middle grades (grades 6, 7, 8).* Baltimore: Johns Hopkins University, Center on School, Family, and Community Partnerships.

Epstein, J. L., & Sanders, M. G. (1998). What we learn from international studies of school, family, and community partnerships. *Childhood Education, 74,* 392–394.

Epstein, J. L., Sanders, M. G., Clark, L. A., & Van Voorhis, F. (1999, August). *Costs and benefits: School, district, and state funding for programs of school, family, and community partnerships.* Paper presented at the annual meeting of the American Sociological Association, Chicago.

Gándara, P., Gutiérrez, D., & O'Hara, S. (2001/this issue). Planning for the future in rural and urban high schools. *Journal of Education for Students Placed At Risk, 6.*

González, N., Andrade, R., Civil, M., & Moll, L. (2001/this issue). Bridging funds of distributed knowledge: Creating zones of practices in mathematics. *Journal of Education for Students Placed At Risk, 6.*

Henze, R. C. (2001/this issue). Segregated classrooms, integrated intent: How one school struggled to develop positive interethnic relations. *Journal of Education for Students Placed At Risk, 6.*

Moll, L. C., Amanti, C., Neff, D., & González, N. (1992). Funds of knowledge for teaching: Using a qualitative approach to connect homes and classrooms. *Theory Into Practice, 31,* 132–141.

Newmann, F., & Sconzert, K. (2000). *School improvement with external partners.* Chicago: Consortium on Chicago School Research.

Plank, S. B. (2000). *Finding one's place: Teaching styles and peer relations in diverse classrooms.* New York: Teachers College Press.

Resnick, M., Bearman, P., Blum, R., Bauman, K., Harris, K., Jones, J., Tabor, J., Beuhring, T., Sieving, R., Shew, M., Ireland, M., Bearinger, L., & Udry, R. (1997). Protecting adolescents from harm: Findings from the national longitudinal study of adolescent health. *Journal of the American Medical Association, 278,* 823–832.

Sanders, M. G. (1999). School membership in the National Network of Partnership Schools: Progress, challenges and next steps. *The Journal of Educational Research, 92,* 220–230.

Sanders, M. G. (in press). Collaborating for student success: A study of the role of "community" in comprehensive programs of school–family–community partnership. *Elementary School Journal.*

Sanders, M. G., & Epstein, J. L. (2000). The National Network of Partnership Schools: How research influences educational practice. *Journal of Education for Students Placed At Risk, 5,* 61–76.

Sanders, M. G., & Harvey, A. (2000, April). *Developing comprehensive programs of school, family, and community partnerships: The community perspective.* Paper presented at the annual meeting of the American Educational Research Association, New Orleans, LA.

JOURNAL OF EDUCATION FOR STUDENTS PLACED AT RISK, 6(1&2), 169–170

NOTES ON CONTRIBUTORS

CAROLYN TEMPLE ADGER is a senior researcher at the Center for Applied Linguistics in Washington, DC. Her research focuses on language in education.

ROSI ANDRADE works with women and children through literature-related activities that promote not only literacy but, more importantly, personal development and consciousness raising.

MARGARITA AZMITIA is an associate professor of psychology at the University of California, Santa Cruz.

MARTA CIVIL is an associate professor of mathematics education at the University of Arizona. Her research interests are teacher education and social and cultural aspects of mathematics education.

FRANCINE F. COLLIGNON is a senior coordinator at the Education Alliance, Brown University.

CATHERINE R. COOPER is professor of psychology and education at the University of California, Santa Cruz, and Director of the Program on Families, Peers, Schools and Communities of the Center for Research on Education, Diversity and Excellence (CREDE).

JANE DURÁN is a research associate at the Graduate School of Education, University of California, Santa Barbara, and a fellow in the Department of Philosophy.

RICHARD P. DURÁN is a professor at the Graduate School of Education, University of California, Santa Barbara.

JOYCE L. EPSTEIN is principal research scientist at the Center for Social Organization of Schools at the Johns Hopkins University. She directs the Center on School, Family, and Community Partnership Schools. Her research focuses on the organization and effects of school, district, and state policies and programs of family and community involvement.

PATRICIA GÁNDARA is professor of education at the University of California, Davis, and Associate Director at the University of California, Linguistic Minority Research Institute.

GIL N. GARCÍA is a Senior Research Analyst in the U.S. Department of Education, Office of Educational Research and Improvement, National Institute on the Education of At Risk Students. He is the CREDE institutional monitor, manages the Southwest Development Educational Laboratory, and is heading the recently launched partnership between OERI and NICHD/NIH on the Development of English Literacy in Spanish-Speaking Children initiative.

NORMA GONZÁLEZ is an associate research anthropologist at the Bureau of Applied Research in Anthropology at the University of Arizona.

DIANNA GUTIÉRREZ is a PhD student in the Division of Education at the University of California, Davis.

ROSEMARY HENZE is an educational anthropologist and Director of research and evaluation at ARC Associates in Oakland, California.

MAKNA MEN is a senior specialist/equity coordinator at the Education Alliance, Brown University, and a certified guidance counselor.

LUIS C. MOLL is a professor in the Department of Language, Reading and Culture, College of Education, University of Arizona. He has conducted educational research with language minority students for the past 20 years. His most recent study is a longitudinal analysis of biliteracy development and the broader social and ideological conditions that mediate such development.

SUSAN O'HARA received her PhD in 2000 from the Division of Education at the University of California, Davis, and is faculty member of California State University at Sacramento.

DEBORAH PERRY-ROMERO is a PhD candidate at the Graduate School of Education, UCSB. She is sponsored by a fellowship from CONACYT, Mexico, where she is a lecturer at the Autonomous University of Queretaro. Her research interests include bilingual language and literacy development.

EDITH SANCHEZ is a graduate student at the Graduate School of Education, University of California, Santa Barbara.

SEREI TAN is a research assistant at the Education Alliance, Brown University, and a social worker in the Providence, Rhode Island school district.

Subscription Order Form

Please ❑ enter ❑ renew my subscription to:

JOURNAL OF EDUCATION FOR
STUDENTS PLACED AT RISK

Volume 6, 2001, Quarterly
1082-4669

Subscription prices per volume:

Individual: ❑ $40.00 US/Canada   ❑ $70.00 All Other Countries

Institution: ❑ $245.00 US/Canada   ❑ $275.00 All Other Countries

Electronic Only: ❑ $36.00 Individual   ❑ $220.50 Institution

Subscriptions are entered on a calendar-year basis only and must be paid in advance in U.S. currency—check, credit card, or money order. Prices for subscriptions include postage and handling. Journal prices expire 12/31/01. NOTE: Institutions must pay institutional rates. Individual subscription orders are welcome if prepaid by credit card or personal check. **Electronic access is available at no additional cost to full-price print subscribers. Electronic-only subscriptions are available at a reduced price.**

❑ Check Enclosed (U.S. Currency Only)

    Total Amount Enclosed $_____

❑ Charge My: ❑ VISA   ❑ MasterCard   ❑ AMEX   ❑ Discover

Card Number _____Exp. Date__________

Signature _____
(Credit card orders cannot be processed without your signature.)

PRINT CLEARLY for proper delivery. STREET ADDRESS/SUITE/ROOM # REQUIRED FOR DELIVERY.

Name _____

Address _____

_____

City _____ State _____ Zip+4 _____
Prices are subject to change without notice.

Please note: A $20.00 penalty will be charged against customers providing checks that must be returned for payment. This assessment will be made only in instances when problems in collecting funds are directly attributable to customer error.

For information about online subscriptions, visit our website at *www.erlbaum.com*

LAWRENCE ERLBAUM ASSOCIATES, INC.
JOURNAL SUBSCRIPTION DEPARTMENT
10 INDUSTRIAL AVENUE, MAHWAH, NJ 07430
(201) 236–9500   FAX: (201) 760–3735
TOLL-FREE: 1–800–926–6579